The New Librarianship Field Guide

The New Librarianship Field Guide

R. David Lankes
with contributions from Wendy Newman, Sue Kowalski, Beck Tench, and
Cheryl Gould
and guidance from the New Librarianship Collaborative: Kimberly Silk,
Wendy Newman, and Lauren Britton

The MIT Press
Cambridge, Massachusetts
London, England

This book was set in Stone Sans Std and Stone Serif Std by Toppan Best-set Premedia Limited. Printed and bound in the United States of America.

Library of Congress Cataloging-in-Publication Data

Names: Lankes, R. David, 1970– author.
Title: The new librarianship field guide / R. David Lankes.
Description: Cambridge, MA ; London, England : The MIT Press, [2015] | Includes
    bibliographical references and index.
Identifiers: LCCN 2015039943 | ISBN 9780262529082 (pbk. : alk. paper)
Subjects: LCSH: Library science—Philosophy. | Libraries and community. | Libraries
    and society. | Librarians—Attitudes.
Classification: LCC Z665 .L375 2015 | DDC 020.1—dc23 LC record available at
    http://lccn.loc.gov/2015039943

10 9 8 7 6 5 4 3 2 1

This book is dedicated to the librarians of Paris and Ferguson. It is dedicated to the librarians of Alexandria and Baltimore. It is dedicated to the librarians in Beirut and New York City. It is dedicated to those librarians who show us that librarians chose to make a difference.

These librarians call us all to stand against the terror and the ignorance and the hopelessness of violence and destruction. These librarians show us the response to man's inhumanity to man should be in knowledge, community, and a rededication to fight prejudice. They show us that in the darkest times knowledge can shine a light.

Contents

Acknowledgments

My heartfelt thanks go out to Wendy Newman, Kim Silk, and Lauren Britton: the New Librarianship Collaborative. Their prompting moved me from recovering from fighting cancer back to advocating for better librarians and better libraries.

My thanks also to Steve Thomas, Lane Wilkinson, and Scott Walter for donating their time and ideas. We don't always agree, but we always seek to learn.

And last but far from least, I want to thank the many librarians and library students who shared their stories, their ideas, and their time to advance my thinking on the field and in the writing of this guide.

The field of librarianship is a noble one, but also one that at times dwells too long on negatives and personalities. It's too easy to become discouraged by venomous exchanges over Twitter, by colleagues' fixation on who are the real movers and shakers in our profession, and by the tendency of some to equate rock star status with having a target on your back.

However, as I found in writing *The Atlas of New Librarianship*, when you look past fads and insecurities, more and more you find the field led by pioneers not only of genius and influence but also of goodwill and passion. It is this passion and the desire to make a difference that pushed me to complete this volume and to continue the quest for world domination through librarianship.

The Field Guide Online

This guide is part of a larger conversation about librarianship, one that gives rise to new tools, new resources, and new ways of convening all the time. To be part of this conversation and get access to expanded materials for these chapters, go to

http://www.NewLibrarianship.org

There you will find videos, articles, blog posts, and other resources to enhance the guide and to better prepare you for improving society through librarianship.

1 Librarianship—Full Stop

Core Chapter Concept: Librarians are agents for radical positive change who choose to make a difference.

I began the introduction to library science class I teach in the summer of 2014 with a story:

The Arab Spring had come to Egypt. In early 2011, on the heels of a successful revolution in Tunisia, Egyptians took to the streets to demand reforms from a regime that had been in power for nearly thirty years. Although the media largely fixated on the protesters who occupied Tahrir Square in the Egyptian capital of Cairo, many protests started in the port city of Alexandria, where, as in Cairo, people from all generations and socioeconomic backgrounds protested to demand liberty, justice, and social equity. In an attempt to restore the constitution, what was seen primarily as a peaceful uprising led to the death of at least 846 people and the injury of an additional 6,000 across Egypt.[1] On January 28 at 6 p.m., after the prisons had opened, releasing murderers and rapists, all security forces withdrew, and gangs of looters roved the streets of Alexandria to take advantage of the resulting chaos.

In Egypt's chief port city, the violence and looting devastated government buildings. Where offices once stood, only burned-out rubble remained. Protesters went from building to building, pulling down the symbols of corrupt power. Some looters and protesters then began to eye the Library of Alexandria.

President Mubarak, the focus of the uprising, had built the modern library in 2002 at a cost of about $220 million, to "recapture the spirit of openness and scholarship of the original,"[2] the famous ancient Library of Alexandria—one of the marvels of the ancient world.

When it became apparent that the library might be in danger, protesters joined hands and surrounded it. Their goal was not to attack the library or to raid it, but to protect it. And, indeed, throughout the protests and looting, the protesters—men, women, and children—stood firm and did protect the library. In essence, they were retaking the library for the people. Even after the uprising subsided, President Mubarak stepped down, and the protesters were celebrating their victory around the country, not a window of the library was broken, and not a rock was thrown against its walls. Why, in the midst of tearing down the regime, did the people of Alexandria protect their library?

My answer was that, over the years, the librarians had been a service to the community and become part of the community—not simply a service of a government seen as disconnected and corrupt. I went on to say the reason the library was unscathed was not that the librarians inside it were exceptional, but rather that they did their job. To be clear, they were brave and brilliant, but to call them "exceptional" is to expect too little of every other librarian. This was the bar, I argued, that all librarians should strive toward.

When I tell this story to students or practicing librarians, I'm met with an unspoken fearful question: "Would I be expected to support a revolution or take part in an uprising?" I would respond with a lighthearted joke to set my audience at ease and move on.

Among those attending that summer 2014 class was Jennifer Ilardi, who also worked in the Florissant Valley Branch of the Saint Louis County Public Library. Turns out that the Florissant Valley Branch serves the same school district that the Ferguson Public Library does in Ferguson, Missouri. After the class ended, Jennifer got on a plane and went home. And then a white policeman shot and killed an unarmed black teenager in Ferguson and the city exploded.

A militarized police force—clad in body armor, helmets, and camouflage uniforms—shot rubber bullets and tear gas at the protesters. Children huddled in their homes, unable to sleep as their parents took turns watching the front door for trouble, and their fathers sat next to a baseball bat "just in case." The Missouri governor called up the State Police and National Guard, announced curfews, and closed governmental institutions.

Such were the disturbing reports out of Ferguson. Disturbing because this was not happening overseas, but in the suburbs of the U.S. heartland.

Issues of justice, race, and economic disadvantage had jumped from the shadows to the forefront of America's consciousness. Yet, in the images of tear-gassed protesters and armored police transports, another story emerged: with the closure of most public institutions in Ferguson, the children of the town were out of school.

This was not just a matter of a delayed school year, but, for many of the low-income families, this was a matter of not having enough to eat. A large percentage of Ferguson's youths received food assistance through the schools. When the city's schools were closed, these children went hungry—trapped in their homes with the sounds of gunfire and exploding tear gas canisters outside.

The Florissant Valley Branch of the Saint Louis County Library and the Ferguson Public Library, which share coverage of the Ferguson-Florissant School District, stepped up to help. In showing their bravery, the staffs of both libraries also showed that librarians could be agents for radical positive change.

Jennifer Ilardi came into her library on Tuesday, August 19, and decided to set up a variety of art supplies in the library's auditorium so that parents could get out of the house, socialize, and create. She also decided to order pizza. During a TV interview, when prompted with "So you saw a need in the community. You saw a void," she replied, "This is what libraries do. We supplement our educational system regularly with after-school programs and summer programs. We provided free lunches all summer long through a collaboration with Operation Food Search because we recognize that a large portion of our community qualifies for free or reduced-price lunches."

With the help of Operation Food Search, the librarians continued to provide these lunches until the schools of Ferguson were reopened. The Magic House, a local children's museum, offered free interactive educational activities for students. Local artists volunteered their services as well, putting on free magic shows. Scott Bonner, director of the Ferguson Public Library down the street from one of the closed schools, teamed up with its teachers to hold classes in the library. When they ran out of room, the librarians connected with local churches and youth centers to arrange a new, impromptu school. Part of this collaboration was the library reaching out, and part was others wanting to get involved. The important thing is that the library had established and maintained these relationships with the community in the past, so it was able to respond quickly.

When I tweeted some of this story, one librarian responded, "A library always makes the difference!" Though I love the activist spirit behind this response (that libraries *make* a difference), I have to disagree with the comment for two reasons. One, it's not libraries but librarians—and, more broadly, library staff—that make a difference. It was a decision that Jennifer, Scott, and their colleagues made to do something. It was their choice to actually help. And, two, sadly, not all librarians *do* make a difference. Some librarians see adherence to policy or not taking sides as reasons to step back from issues and even from outright breakdowns in the social order. Still others limit their views by asking, "How can our library collection and reading address a problem of civil unrest?" Librarians can make a difference, but to do so, we must hold a proactive view of our profession and our communities.

Too many librarians see our profession as a passive occupation: they stay safely in the background, ready to serve, but only within their libraries. That is wrong. Good librarians, the kind our communities need, see our profession as a chance not just to promote reading or inform their communities, but also to make a positive difference there. They see their mission as the improvement of society. They see the role of librarians and their institutions as addressing the issues that have exploded in Ferguson, not with tear gas and rubber bullets, but with free lunches, magic shows, and, above all, with learning.

Some may see summer programs and free lunches as ineffectual tools in comparison to tear gas and body armor in dealing with violence, but they are wrong. An engaged community with librarians dedicated to learning and making a difference—the promise of opportunity and a better tomorrow, rather than the threat of force—is a powerful deterrent to violence.

Thus the purpose of this guide is to prepare librarians to be agents for radical positive change and to directly engage their communities—be these scholars, students, lawyers, residents, or bureaucrats—to use knowledge to achieve their dreams and aspirations. Some may find the word "radical" problematic. To some, it implies civil disobedience and an adherence to a far-left ideology. Surely, by using the term "radical" some believe I am advocating transforming librarians into political leftists at odds with their roles in civic, academic, school, and business institutions. But this is a wrong interpretation of the word "radical" in this context.

Indeed, to some, a "radical" is a violent extremist, someone who seeks the outright destruction of governments and who is dedicated to using violence to achieve political or social aims, often associated with a given religion. This, too, is a wrong interpretation of "radical" for the context.

Both interpretations of "radical" (as leftist or violent extremist) are one-dimensional uses of the term. Both have a long history with complex associations: struggles for rights or domination or disruption across a broad political spectrum. "Radical" has been used to marginalize or target a segment of the population. Some wear "radical" as a badge of honor, whereas, to others, it's a label of shame.

According to the *Oxford English Dictionary* the word radical has four distinct meanings:[3]

1. Far-reaching, or thorough in relation to change (a radical shift in an organization's strategy)

2. Advocating complete social reform (the radical leftists called for reform of the electoral system)

3. Something fundamental or at the root of things (a radical mastectomy removes the entire mammary gland)

4. Very good or excellent (that movie was radical!)

Merriam-Webster's has these four definitions as well:[4]

1. "of, relating to, or proceeding from a root"

2. "of or relating to the origin: fundamental"

3. "very different from the usual or traditional: extreme"

4. "slang: excellent, cool"

In labor movements, "radical" is often compressed to "advocating for fundamental changes." In geopolitics, it's flattened to "extreme." Yet "radical" is a word that means "extreme," "fundamental," "thorough," and "cool"—all at the same time. To me, it's the perfect description of the type of librarianship I seek to instill in my readers—professionals advocating and enabling far-reaching change based on deeply held principles in an exciting way. This is not a new concept of librarianship. Indeed, you could argue that the adoption of issues such as intellectual freedom, privacy, and a host of ethical stances has been a hallmark of librarianship from its very beginnings and that adopting such issues is "radical" in all senses of the word.

That said, the discourse of this approach to librarianship has given rise to confusion and downright animosity over the use of the term "radical." Some have implied that the term, with its encompassing rhetoric of improving society, calls up visions of jackbooted librarians storming a community to enforce a special sense of social justice. Nothing could be further from the truth. Librarians engage communities in a discussion of just what "improving" entails; librarians are a part of that conversation, representing values and principles developed over millennia. It's telling that, in many situations (broad indiscriminate surveillance of citizens, censorship, the erosion of privacy in the marketplace), it is librarians who have stood against the forces of oligarchy and the trampling of the rights of minorities and the disenfranchised. They've done so not out of an allegiance to some liberal agenda, but as a commitment to democratic principles and transparency. One thing that's common across all these uses of "radical" is implied action: whether political or institutional, or simply how you behave and comport yourself. To be radical is to seek action and change.

The New Language of Librarianship

In some ways, this entire book is about vocabulary and the use of words. Just as "radical" is more than a set of definitions, "librarian," "library," and "librarianship" are terms enmeshed in cultural discourse. For many, these words have seemingly clear definitions. Yet, as we'll see, when these definitions and our beliefs are put to the test, they often come up wanting. So we'll seek to decode these terms, link them to deeper understandings and, ultimately, to practice. Before getting too far into our discussion of librarians and librarianship, however, it's important to put forth some clear definitions of key terms that will be used repeatedly.

"New Librarianship"

There's an old joke that goes, "Folks in tech support never say no; they simply throw acronyms at you until you go away: 'Well, we could set up your blog, but we would have to install PHP on our NAS and make a special entry in the NAT and DHCP tables to allow for a ...'"

I've found there is an equivalent joke in the librarian profession: "Librarians never say no; they simply tell you how great your ideas would be implemented in a different type of library: 'What a great idea for a [public

| academic | special | government | small | large | urban | rural] library.'"
(Pick any one of these as long as it's not *your* library.) I believe it's why we
use so many modifiers in the field: "digital" library, "virtual" reference,
"patron-driven" acquisition, and so on. Yes, we often use them to find like
minds, but many times we also use them to set ourselves apart. The same
has been true of the phrase "New Librarianship." What few of those librarians who follow my work realize is that I never intended New Librarianship
to become a special type of librarianship. The whole point of *The Atlas of
New Librarianship* (almost named *The New Atlas of Librarianship*) was not to
create some special form of librarianship, but rather to build a foundation
for change across the entire profession.

I want to reemphasize that decision here because there are many who
talk about New Librarianship as if it's a special type of librarianship, often
as a way to dismiss it. Some have said, "New librarianship is all about communities, so it's really just for public libraries." *All* libraries, whether public
or private, large or small, should be about communities, those they serve
and are part of—that's just librarianship.

"New librarianship," it's been said, "is fine for big libraries that can
afford outreach staff and who aren't busy organizing materials." But engaging and improving communities are best done in tight partnership with
those communities. Who better to foster such partnership than librarians
in small communities with their greater knowledge of those who need their
services? Some of the most innovative librarians on the planet serve communities from four to a thousand people. And librarians can engage larger
communities in all services—from cataloging to checkout.

"New Librarianship is great for librarians in libraries, but I'm a con-
sultant [embedded librarian | information specialist | vendor employee |
freelancer | jobber]." Librarians fulfill their mission in all contexts and serve
as the fundamental unit for the community approach to librarianship.
Librarians might build and maintain libraries, but they ultimately build
better communities with or without an actual or virtual place called a
"library."

Bottom line: this guide is about librarianship. Period. Full stop.

Although a new approach to librarians and libraries, the community
approach is built on the foundation of librarianship built over millennia.
It's not the first time librarians have sought to reframe their work (Melvil
Dewey and S. R. Ranganathan come immediately to mind), and it won't

be the last. Librarianship grows and adapts to the present because it adopts
and adapts the social constructs of the communities it serves. As these
communities (universities, schools, law firms) change, so, too, must
librarianship.

"Member"

I will not speak of "users" because our communities are part of what we
do, and librarians are not tools to be sucked dry of value and discarded.[5]
Nor will I speak of "patrons" because we should be energized by our communities, not patronized by them. I will definitely not use the term "consumers" or "customers" because we are part of the communities we serve,
not providers of services to be bought and sold. The value we bring is not
immediately reducible to dollars and cents because it is so intertwined in
the future well-being of our communities. Don't get me wrong, there are
times when, acting as individuals or on behalf of our institutions, each
of us will need to calculate how well money is spent, but that's not at all
the same as defining our professional identity as a cost in someone's
spreadsheet.

I will use the term "member" and, more often than not, "community
member." Although it has a connotation of exclusion (if there are members, there must also be nonmembers), "member" is meant to emphasize
belonging and shared ownership (and responsibility). Which is not to
imply that the term will fit in all circumstances. Thus, in an academic
context, it just makes sense to refer to faculty and students as, well, "faculty" and "students." Some public libraries use the term "neighbor" (I love
that). The term we use within the profession should in no way limit how
we use terminology to interact with our communities. I, for one, prefer to
be called "David" rather than "member" when I work with my fellow
librarians.

"Community"

Asking, "A member of what?" takes us to my last key term. The answer, of
course, is "a community." I use the word "community" a lot. In fact, community is central to librarianship. Many might mistake this as a focus on
public libraries. A community, as will be further defined later, is not limited
to a community of citizens in a given geographical location. Employees
of a law firm constitute a community. A university is a community of

students, scholars, staff, and administrators. Doctors are a professional community. Students, teachers, parents, and principals make up the community of a school. It comes down to the root of "community"—the Latin *communitas*: a group of people sharing possessions and responsibilities. This applies to all communities; be those possessions a building, a tax ID, a plot of land, or a set of values.

Acknowledging the Atlas in the Room

What you hold in your hands is the tip of a proverbial iceberg: an accessible portion of a much larger whole. Beneath the waves of summary and application is a much deeper well of theory and argument. Beneath the surface lies the work of scholars and reflective practitioners recreating librarianship around core values and the communities they serve.

That said, this guide was written both for readers new to the community approach to librarianship and for those who have read *The Atlas of New Librarianship*. In building on the basic concepts of librarianship discussed in greater depth in the *Atlas*, it offers specific tools to implement transformative change in your libraries and communities. It also offers deeper understandings to help you redefine what a library is, and what services it should provide.

Structure of the Guide

The guide has three main parts:

1. "Librarians": a discussion of the mission of librarians, their values, and their means of facilitating knowledge creation;
2. "Libraries": a discussion of what a library is in a time of makerspaces, lending of fishing poles, and community as collection; and
3. "Excursus: From Mission to Missionary": a discussion and set of tools to promote a librarianship centered on community aspirations and abilities.

Where possible, I've provided specific examples—meant to inspire not duplicate. I have also invited several contributors to add their experiences. Throughout I have kept notes and references to a minimum to ease readability. In the discussion points for most chapters at the end of the guide,

I've invited you to add to the text through your own examples, arguments, and alternative views. And for most chapters, I've included additional reading there as well; these resources provide ample citations to related works for you to pursue and will, I hope, lead to deeper discussions of the concepts presented in the main text.

So with our task outlined, let us begin with a question, "What exactly is a librarian?"

Librarians

2 They Named the Building after Us

Core Chapter Concept: Define libraries by the work of librarians—not the other way around.

What is a librarian? This seems like an innocuous question and a logical place to start in a book about librarianship. But for many people this is backwards. Many scholars and library science educators start by defining a library (or, more often than not, by assuming that everyone has the same definition of a library) and, from that, derive the definition of "librarian." This paradigm of defining librarians and librarianship in terms of libraries is found in library literature and certainly in the larger public discourse.

Look at how the *Oxford Pocket Dictionary of Current English* defines "librarian": "a person, typically with a degree in library science, who administers or assists in a library."[1]

The definition is simple enough. Except, of course, that it doesn't work. And it doesn't work three reasons:

1. What about those who have a degree in library science but who *don't* work in a library? There are plenty of librarians who work for publishers, banks, and a whole cadre who work for companies such as Elsevier, Online Computer Library Center, Inc. (OCLC), and even Google.

2. The word "typically" is problematic because there are plenty of people who have the title of "librarian" with no professional degree. Are they *less* librarians than those who have a master's degree? Is *anyone* who works in a library a librarian, like the security guard or custodian?

3. This definition assumes we know what a library is, a dubious assumption in these days of makerspaces and Little Free Libraries.

And when you consider that the definition makes no mention of the ultimate beneficiaries of that person's work, the community or a community member, its inadequacy becomes all the more obvious. How do you prepare, or manage, or evaluate a librarian when what that person does, why, for whom, and how are ultimately ungrounded?

We can see an implicit definition of librarians by their relation to institutional libraries, in the Code of Ethics of the American Library Association:

We [librarians] provide the highest level of service to all library users through appropriate and usefully organized resources; equitable service policies; equitable access; and accurate, unbiased, and courteous responses to all requests.[2]

So does that mean if librarians work in settings other than libraries, they *don't* have to provide the "highest level of service" or be courteous? Many people have attempted to solve the problem of defining "librarian" by developing new terms: "information professional," for example. Except that there are plenty of professionals who work with information (a concept we'll return to again and again) but who have no idea what it means to be a librarian. Bottom line: defining librarians in relation to an ungrounded concept of library presents a whole series of problems.

One huge problem with this approach is what I call the "functional view" of the profession, that is, defining librarians by what they do. Thus librarians are people who organize things. Of course, so are retailers, lawyers, and even four-year-olds. Or librarians are people who search through large collections of information to find things. But so are forensic specialists, data analysts, and genealogists.

Now many of you are saying something to the effect of "Thou doth protest too much." After all, just as a given word, like "radical," can span plenty of meanings, so a given skill can span plenty of professions. We simply "know" a librarian or library when we see one. Let's face it, if you're reading this, you either are or want to be a librarian. But being ungrounded in our definitions of both "librarian" and "library" has a major consequence when it comes to accommodating change.

Institutions, organizations, and professions all have one thing in common: to survive, they must change. They must adapt to new societal and economic conditions (including the changing marketplace of ideas). They must identify and handle threats even as they identify and act on opportunities. Take, for example, farmers.

Farming and farmers are around today not because they do what farmers have done since demise of the hunter-gatherer monopoly, but because they have found new ways to work the land and meet the needs of an ever-growing global population. Farmers today may have a kinship with medieval farmers of the eighth century, but they also have access to pest-resistant seed stock, combines, synthetic fertilizers, and so on. The tools of farming have changed; its purpose has not. So, too, librarians today may have a kinship with Egyptian librarians of the third century BC, but they use a wide range of new technologies to serve their communities and the larger society.

The key here is to identify what's unchanging and what's changeable in librarianship. I argue that librarians' mission, values, and means of facilitation provide the grounding of librarianship and are unchanging, whereas librarians' tools (books, scrolls, e-book readers, 3-D printers, buildings, cataloging, reference) are changeable. We therefore define librarianship based on *why* we do things to accomplish our mission in accordance with our values and not on *how* we do them.

You may rightly ask where the mission, values, and means of facilitation come from? Are they historical holdovers, or are they grounded in something more solid? After all, libraries of whatever kind are made by people. There's no natural law governing their operation, structure, or goals. We can't develop a theory of librarianship as astronomers can a theory of star formation. We might just as soon develop a theory of British Petroleum.

The very short answer is that librarians' mission, as we'll soon discuss, comes from a social agreement between librarians and the communities they serve that's been reaffirmed century after century. The values come from a long-standing history of implementing that mission. And the means of facilitation comes from how people learn and create knowledge—the core of the mission of librarians. In this guide, we'll look at all three of these in great detail (all three are discussed in still greater detail in *The Atlas of New Librarianship*). We'll start with the mission of librarians.

3   The Mission of Librarians

Core Chapter Concept: The mission of librarians is to improve society through facilitating knowledge creation in their communities.

What's the importance of a mission statement? Ideally, it provides both direction to a group and a benchmark to test new activities and concepts against. The mission of librarians presented above is short and sweet, yet hidden within it is a huge set of connected ideas, many of which will be unraveled in the first part of this guide.

A Very Brief History of Libraries

Let's begin by asking where this mission comes from. Although the wording is mine, the core of it comes from a long-standing agreement between those who run libraries and the communities they serve. As far back as the ancient Library of Alexandria in the third century BC, libraries were built as places to learn and advance knowledge. Throughout Muslim Spain in the eleventh century, libraries were built and run to advance society's understanding of mathematics, engineering, and the human condition. In the Middle Ages, newly emerging universities built libraries as an aid to both scholars and students. Many of these academic libraries were run by scholars as a sort of laboratory for their research. In the nineteenth century, public libraries emerged in the United States as part of the public education movement. Andrew Carnegie thought of libraries as "the people's university"; he built them around the world to ensure that people who governed themselves were educated.

The point is that, however closely libraries have been associated with collections, the items collected were almost always tools to serve a higher purpose. The tools have changed and evolved, from clay tablets to wooden carvings to papyrus scrolls to parchment manuscripts to paper books to digital resources, but the librarians' mission to improve society through knowledge has remained the same. Certainly, the idea of who could improve society (royalty, white males, the privileged, the masses) has also changed, yet it's always been the mission of libraries and those who built and maintained them to educate.

Other parts of the stated mission of librarians have also changed over time. For example, the very idea of what constitutes a librarian. In ancient Egypt, the librarians of Alexandria were close advisors to the kings and queens. From the Middle Ages until the guild movements of the 1800s, they were often historians or monks who used the libraries as their own laboratories or clerks who maintained the libraries. In more recent days, librarians were defined as people who worked in institutions called "librar-ies." The profession of librarian, as recognized today, began with the move-ments, first, to form professional guilds and, later, to form labor unions. The role of librarian has continued to evolve with the requirement of higher education degrees (first a bachelor's and later a master's), although many earn the title of "librarian" simply by their employment. Yet, through all of this history, the librarians, historians, monks, and clerks in libraries have sought a better tomorrow through learning and knowledge.

As my very brief history of libraries clearly suggests, much of the history of our profession has been told from an institutional perspective. A large reason for this guide is the need, with the emergence of librarians as profes-sionals and their growing ability to do the work of improving society through knowledge creation outside any institutional or physical library, to ground librarianship in something other than a place. It is time not to formulate a new mission, but to explicitly tie this mission to the people who do the work in any context. Today, librarians work in banks and tech companies; they are freelance software programmers; they provide services not just in libraries, but in parking lots and ice rinks and online.

A Two-Part Mission

It is important to note that the mission statement I put forth has two distinct parts. The first sets an objective, "to improve society"; the second, the means to achieve that objective, "through facilitating knowledge cre-ation in their communities." Both are essential. The objective (to improve society) acts as an ethical counterbalance to the means (facilitating knowledge creation). So librarians help people learn, but they shape that learning around the goals of their communities and societies. A librarian working in a public library may provide only the thinnest of services around the topic of cosmology or particle physics. However, a librarian embedded in a research team of the CERN Large Hadron Collider would work to provide greater resources and services on that topic to his or her team.

Please note, too, that this mission is the mission of *librarians*, not of libraries or any specific library. As organizations, libraries should have clear missions as well, but these should vary greatly based upon the communities they seek to serve. On the other hand, no matter how different the missions of their libraries, the mission of the *librarians* remains the same—improving society through facilitating knowledge creation. That the missions for libraries and librarians differ makes sense since, as will be discussed, libraries as institutions must reflect the unique aspirations and characteristics of individual communities, whereas librarians must be able to function as professionals across a wide range of contexts.

This brings us to another important characteristic about the mission—it rests upon a worldview—a rich network of shared experience, assumptions, and values both stated and implied that represents how an individual or group understands the world. And worldviews can and do differ, of course, sometimes by quite a lot. For example, there are some who claim that the very idea of a mission for librarians is problematic; they point out that a mission implies an agenda and that there is a strong historical narrative of librarians being neutral or unbiased. These people would argue that if you're a librarian, your mission is solely defined by the community, organization, or institution you serve. If you're hired by a town, then the town defines your mission. If you're hired by a state or a company or a university, then your mission is the mission of that state or company or university. This argument is often extended to public servants of all sorts: from legislators to town clerks to members of zoning boards. I call this worldview the "servant model." It's the idea that, as a librarian, you carry out the will of the people you serve dispassionately without letting ideology or personal views color your work.

In contrast, the mission presented here is based on a worldview that might be best called the "stewardship model." In this worldview, part of the worth of professionals is their values and perspectives. Good librarians aren't neutral: they are principled. Their work is about making things better, and therefore they must have a belief in what is better. This idea is far from universal or taken as a fact, as will be discussed in chapter 4 ("Knowledge Creation") and chapter 7 ("Improve Society").

For example, good librarians value intellectual freedom. This is a belief that the best learning occurs in the richest environment of inputs (books, people, ideas). This is not some universal truth, and it directly opposes models of management and governance that seek to restrict disclosure to the "right information." This can be seen in restrictions placed on the Internet in China and in the regulation of business practices and campaign finance in the United States. In these instances, the argument is made that the best decisions are made in the presence of the "right" information. So if librarians value intellectual freedom, they are hardly neutral or dispassionate.

Our Mission Is Not Unique

Our mission, to improve society through facilitating knowledge creation, is not unique to librarians. Teachers and professors could easily lay claim to this mission. Publishers and even Google employees could claim it as their own. Our mission is vital, but insufficient to uniquely identify or guide our profession. To it, we must add (as we will in later chapters) our means of facilitation and our values. So teachers may have the same mission, but tend to facilitate knowledge creation very differently (through structured curricula, mediated facilitation, and strong assessment). Google may be an important tool in knowledge creation, but those tools are driven by profit rather than stewardship.

So hold dear our mission, but understand that if that is all you present to the world, it will cause great confusion. Why do we need librarians when we have Google? Why shouldn't the curriculum and class structure of in-classroom teachers be applied directly to school librarians? Why hire librarians when there are plenty of people with Ph.D.s out there who are more familiar with a given topic? These questions arise because of an incomplete understanding of the true nature of librarianship.

Stand for Something or Fall for Everything

Here's the easy takeaway from this chapter: we librarians have a mission as professionals that guides our actions and cements our value. That mission is both about what we do (facilitate knowledge creation) and why we do it (to improve society). That mission, however recent its phrasing, is long standing in intent and provides a kinship with those who have built and maintained libraries through the ages; it continues today inside and outside the confines of a library.

But what seems easy requires something much harder, as will be discussed throughout this guide. It requires, first, a deep understanding of what is meant by "improvement," "knowledge," and even "communities." It also requires a strong and thoughtful examination of our mission in practice. Take something as simple as telling someone how to bypass Internet filters implemented by a particular library. On the one hand, by doing so, you're helping that person increase his or her knowledge. The website being filtered may be an important source of information on an important topic (people may be denied access to useful information about breast cancer because sites providing such information are filtered for containing the word "breast" with images of breasts, or access to information that might help them identify and avoid hate groups because the sites of such groups are also filtered). On the other hand, by doing so, you're also going against the stated policies of the institution you work for—a surrogate of the larger community. Or you may inadvertently be showing someone how to circumvent filters for illegal file sharing, and so on. The point here (and the whole point of this guide) is that knowing your mission is only a start and *must* be matched by deeper reflection and personal commitment to do good.

Every day, librarians enforce copyright policies that we may disagree with and that, in some ways, run contrary to the values of our profession. Every day, librarians must decide between a desire to preserve the privacy of our community members and offering services our communities demand. Every day, librarians must make a choice between doing what's easy, doing what's right, and determining what's right in the first place. No textbook or mission statement or policy document can relieve us of the necessity to make those decisions, nor remove the complexity of those decisions. That's why we are librarians and why librarians are professionals, not clerks. That's why we are stewards within the communities we serve, not servants to them. That's why we must shape the missions and the work of our organizations and communities, and not simply accept them.

4 Knowledge Creation

Core Chapter Concept: Knowledge is created through conversation—if you're in the knowledge business, you're in the conversation business.

So you're a librarian on a mission to improve society. You are not alone. Police officers seek to improve society, as do firemen, politicians, lawyers, doctors, and teachers, among many others. One of the key things that separate you from many other professions is that you seek to do so with a firm focus on knowledge. That is, a librarian seeks to improve communities and society through making them smarter.

Here again, the relatively simple phrase "making them smarter" has deeper implications. Most texts on librarianship, and indeed most courses on the preparation and continuing education of librarians, jump directly to *how* we make communities smarter: a rich and well-organized collection, reference and research services, readers advisory, and so on. But they often skip over a very important question: what is "smarter" exactly?

Why does that question matter so much? Because it shapes *everything* in the work of librarians and the libraries they have built over the millennia. Take the Dewey Decimal System, Melvil Dewey's—and most public libraries'—way of organizing books by numbers. Well, not all books. For example, there are no Dewey numbers for works of fiction, at least not in the original version of the system. Why? Dewey didn't think libraries should be in the fiction business: libraries were all about learning, and, he believed, you didn't learn from fiction. Disagree? Good. Yet the belief that knowledge comes only from nonfiction resources shaped libraries of all sorts for over a century.

What's more, Dewey believed that all of human knowledge could be represented in a single, unified manner. In essence, he believed that libraries were in the truth business, and that there was a single truth we could all agree on. Simple, right? So then you're okay with the fact that Dewey put cookbooks in with books about business because he thought cooking (or "cookery," as he called it) was a woman's business? How about the fact that, in the 200s for "Religion," he assigned 200–287 to Christian texts, but only 289–299 to all other religious texts (288 is no longer used)? So that, for example, 278 is the number assigned to works of or about the "Christian church in South America," whereas 296 is the number assigned to *all* works of or about Judaism. Do you still feel that libraries using his system are shaped by a single objective truth?

Thus, to be a librarian is not simply about knowing how to do things, but about knowing *why* things are done. And what underlies our knowledge-based profession is the nature of knowledge itself. The way we understand the process of becoming knowledgeable (learning) affects the services we offer, the way we organize resources, the way we evaluate our performance, and ultimately the value we provide as professionals to our communities and to society as a whole. So let's start by disabusing you of a widely held belief that librarians are "information professionals."

Information Is a Lie

There is a good chance you've been told you live in the "Information Age." You have most likely heard about the promise of information technology and how rapid access to information will improve our lives. There is an excellent chance you became a librarian because you saw power in information. Power to control your life and power to improve the lives of others. Yet do you really know what information is? Can you define it? Are the words on this page information? Is the book itself?

Don't be ashamed if you find these questions harder to answer than you thought. I've a Ph.D. in information science and still find it hard to come up with a good definition of "information." It's kind of like a library—you know it when you see it, right?

Now just because I have a hard time coming up with a definition of "information" doesn't mean many smarter people haven't tried. Michael Buckland, for example, didn't just come up with one definition, he came up with three:

1. *Information-as-process*: When someone is informed, what they know is changed. In this sense "information" is "The act of informing ...; communication of the knowledge or 'news' of some fact or occurrence; the action of telling or fact of being told of something" (*Oxford English Dictionary*, 1989, vol. 7, p. 944).

2. *Information-as-knowledge*: "Information" is also used to denote that which is perceived in "information-as-process": the "knowledge communicated concerning some particular fact, subject, or event; that of which one is apprised or told; intelligence, news" (*Oxford English Dictionary*, 1989, vol. 7, p. 944). The notion of information as that which reduces uncertainty could be viewed as a special case of "information-as-knowledge." Sometimes information increases uncertainty.

3. *Information-as-thing*: The term "information" is also used attributively for objects, such as data and documents, that are referred to as "information" because they are regarded as being informative, as "having the quality of imparting knowledge or communicating information; instructive" (*Oxford English Dictionary*, 1989, vol. 7, p. 946).[1]

One of the most widely used definitions of information comes in the form of the DIKW (data-information-knowledge-wisdom) hierarchy,[2] which defines "information" by contrasting it with three other concepts. At the bottom of the hierarchy are the ever-plentiful *data* (singular, "datum"). Data are simply recorded measurements. In today's digital world, these measurements are most often in the form of ones and zeros, but the length of a rope and the temperature outside are also data.

When you add context to data, you get *information*. If I tell you, "It's 1°," that would be a datum because it's a measurement out of context. However, if I say, "It's 1° outside," you would understand I'm talking about temperature. So "1° outside" would be information.

When you connect bits of information, you get *knowledge*. So connecting the bit that it's 1° outside with the bit that 1° is too cold for normal indoor clothing, you know you should dress warmly if you want to go outside or avoid going out altogether.

At the top of the DIKW hierarchy is *wisdom*—more an aspirational goal than a concept with a straightforward definition. Here you can use knowledge to see overall patterns and make "wisest" use of those patterns (like making money selling gloves on the street to the unprepared).

But is the DIKW hierarchy really helpful to a librarian? Even though we can all agree on what data are, what context is can and does differ from one situation or person to another. For example, when I said, "1° outside," did I mean Fahrenheit or Celsius? If I meant 1° Celsius, that would be 34° Fahrenheit or 2 degrees above freezing—time for gloves and a warm coat or jacket, but if I meant 1° Fahrenheit or 31 degrees *below* freezing, chances are you wouldn't be going outside at all. Also, there's the problem of novelty. If I tell you it's 1° outside (let's just assume I mean Fahrenheit since, as an American, the metric system scares) and then someone else tells you the same, are *both* instances information?

It gets worse still. What if I tell you it's 1° outside, but it's actually 30°? If you don't know I'm lying, is it *still* information? What about if you *do* know I'm lying?

Is this book information? If so, how much information? Does it contain the same amount for you, who are reading it for the first time, as it does for me, who wrote it?

Bottom line: talking about "information" is not helpful to a librarian. We can use terms like "information professional" and "informing" all we want, but often these are either surrogates for documents, data, or simply attempts to absolve ourselves of any responsibility for what people do with what we provide.

No, librarians aren't in the information business—we're in the knowledge business, and, as you'll see, that puts us in the *conversation* business, which leads to some rather startling new types of services and practices.

Knowledge, Knowing, and Pragmatism

Philosophers, theologians, and scientists of all stripes have argued about the nature of knowledge for millennia. Throw in terms like "truth" and "belief," and the debates get deeper and longer. In this guide, I'm not going to provide a simple and universally accepted definition of "knowledge" because, frankly, one doesn't exist. Instead, I'll provide a pragmatic framework for approaching learning and knowledge creation in the amazingly diverse communities we interact with.

For librarians, "knowledge" is the set of beliefs held in relation to one another that dictate behaviors. This set is a network constructed through conversations and actions on our own and in larger communities. Note, knowledge is *not* equivalent to absolute truth. Truth is an area of pursuit reserved for philosophers and priests (and apparently for Melvil Dewey as well). Instead, librarians are interested in what people believe, and how this will impact what they do. This is a scientific or rational approach.

If you thought the scientific approach was all about truth, you are not alone. Many take the output of scientific studies as truth. Certainly, the media report it as such. This is why we regularly see headlines about what's good for us (chocolate, coffee, lean red meat), followed months later by headlines that directly contradict those findings. How can scientific truth be so malleable?

Although the scientific method and the underlying philosophy of scientific inquiry are about the *search* for truth, the tools of science, paradoxically, are such that scientists can never declare with absolute certainty whether something is true or not. Take, for a moment, gravity. Clearly, there is something in the universe we call "gravity"—so that's true, right? Except that, when you ask physicists to explain gravity, you'll quickly find out that there's a lot of debate about what gravity really is, and how it works. Further, even though physicists know quite a lot about gravity, the two prevailing paradigms of physics, relativity and quantum mechanics, approach gravity in two separate and incompatible ways. That's right, we understand the physical world around us in two separate and incompatible ways. Which way is true? Probably neither. Which is useful? Both.

Using the scientific or rational method of understanding anything, you observe a phenomenon and create a hypothesis to explain the phenomenon. You test your hypothesis against the data for that phenomenon, and, if it holds up, you eventually develop a theory. A theory, as used in science, is not a guess, but a logical explanation of a phenomenon that can account for all the data. What's the difference between a theory and truth? Every valid scientific theory, from the theory of evolution to the theory of relativity, from the germ theory of disease to the theory of climate change, must be falsifiable—that is, it must be able to be disproved. In science, every theory is considered our best understanding *thus far*. If there's even one datum that can't be explained by the theory, the theory is considered invalid, no matter how useful it might be. That's why theories like the theory of evolution and the germ theory of disease are so important—they have lasted for centuries with plenty of people trying—and failing—to disprove them. On the other hand, it also means that scientists *never* take a theory as truth. It is a working understanding only, a grounded and logically supported belief of how the world operates.

Recorded Knowledge Is a Lie, Too

Before we dive deeper into the nature of knowledge, we need to clear up something we'll come back to again and again. Knowledge is uniquely human, which means you can't write it down and you can't record it. What you have in a book or a file is not knowledge, but an *artifact* of knowledge. Now don't get me wrong, artifacts are very important and have helped to propel us forward through the millennia, but they're still not knowledge.

Take Ayers Rock in the outback of Australia, for example. Geologists can tell you the composition of the rock, its age, even the forces of nature that formed it over time. The aboriginal people can tell you why the rock is an important part of their culture and belief system. But none of this comes from the rock itself. Without knowledge of geology, you couldn't determine the rock's composition or its age. Likewise, without knowledge of aboriginal culture and beliefs, you couldn't read its cultural significance. The knowledge of time and significance is not contained within the rock; it's brought to it by people.

The same is true of a book or article. A book is not knowledge. Just because you can read its words doesn't mean you can make them part of your knowledge. If transferring knowledge from text to brain were that simple, we'd all be brilliant.

As you look at rack upon rack of books in a library, don't think of them as packets of knowledge. Instead, think of them as flints, waiting to spark something unique in each person who encounters them.

So What Is Knowledge?

So if knowledge isn't truth (at least not as "truth" will be used in this guide), then what is it, and how does this affect everything librarians do? The short answer is that "knowledge" is a set of interrelated *agreements* that drive how people act. These agreements are derived through *conversants* using *language* and are held over time in people's *memories*. The agreements dictate our actions, and if, as librarians, we want to follow our mission of improving society through facilitating knowledge creation in our communities, we have to both understand how people come up with these agreements and start with what people know, not with what they should know.

In this section, I'm first going to cover the agreements, memories, and such that make up knowledge. I'm then going to talk about how we create knowledge—how we learn. And I'll finish by discussing what I mean by "start with what people know." Throughout, I'll show you specifically how a knowledge framework shapes our work as librarians.

1 + 1 = Climate Change?

To some of you, the phrase "knowledge creation" in the mission statement set forth in chapter 3 might seem odd, puzzling, or even illogical. After all, most people come to a library or librarian to find some *existing* piece of knowledge, don't they? Not everyone can be a scientist pushing the frontiers of science … right?

Although it may be true that not everyone can be a scientist, everyone does create knowledge all the time. Take something as simple as 1 + 1 = 2. You probably learned this rather early in life, and when you did, you created knowledge.

"Wait! Wait!" you protest. "I may be old, but not that old. I didn't *create* 1 + 1 = 2—it already *was*."

When you added your understanding that 1 + 1 = 2 to how you approached the world, you created a new bit of knowledge for yourself. Take a closer look at this example. When you read 1 + 1 = 2, you assumed the "+" symbol meant "plus" (or "added to"). And you assumed that whoever taught you this was talking about normal counting numbers or the base 10 system. So the fact that you associated 1 + 1 with the base 10 system was your understanding—your view—your creation. And the fact that it was and is widely shared, based on a huge set of social agreements, doesn't make it any less so. When I talk about "creating knowledge," I'm not talking about learning something brand new about some objective reality in the universe, I'm talking about how we learn and react to that reality.

What does this have to do with librarianship? Well, consider the following situation. A grade school student walks up to the reference desk and asks you what's the best way to add two numbers. Absent any indication to the contrary, you can safely assume the student means numbers in base 10. But there's a good chance that the way you learned to add two numbers is different from the way students do today. I learned addition by memorizing addition tables—"sums"—of all number pairs from 1 to 10 (1 + 1 = 2, 1 + 2 = 3, 1 + 3 = 4, and so on; 2 + 1 = 3, 2 + 2 = 4, 2 + 3 = 5, and so on). Today, the emphasis is on number theory and quantities. So today's students learn with grouping blocks, groups of 10s, "friendly numbers," and number lines. And, as a good reference librarian, you would need to know that.[3]

What's more, let's say you're a public librarian serving students from a local school that uses the Common Core math standards.[4] If you simply provide students with answers to their math problems or hand them a number table, you're short-circuiting their schoolwork, and you may well be confusing them. Understanding that knowledge is created within each individual means that, as a librarian, you can't simply assume that everyone starts with the same context, or that there is a single way of knowing something. Librarians must make every effort to understand what an individual or community knows, and build from that point.

Our math example may seem overly simple, so let's make things more interesting. A community member walks into the library and wants information on climate change (or, as we now understand it, wants to "create knowledge on climate change for him- or herself"). Do you provide articles based on the preponderance of scientific evidence for human-caused climate change? If the member is a skeptic, all you may have done is prove to this person that the library and you as a librarian are biased and support a "liberal agenda." Do you provide articles on *both* sides of the debate? Now you've given the impression that both sides of the debate are equally valid.

The realization that knowledge is constructed—created—by an individual is not limited to direct exchanges either. What books do you collect on the topic? What materials do you highlight in digital resources? Do you support changing energy use policies for your organization (library, school, business, research team)? What message does it send to your community, for example, if your library puts solar panels on the roof?

The short answer to all of this is that you must start by understanding where each member is in terms of knowing, and you must be well aware of where you want that member to go from there. When a member asks a question, your first response should be a set of questions of your own, not a Google search. In building a collection development policy for your organization, you should start by surveying the community members who will use that collection, not with the materials available. For example, at a university that has faculty studying climate change, they probably will need materials that oppose the prevailing consensus as much as materials that support it. They'll need to study both to determine whether prevailing theories of climate change still work in the face of contrary data, and they probably will need to understand the public debate when they interact with people outside their domain or the academy.

Now comes the tricky part. You need to know not only where each member is—what that member knows—but where the member needs to go. This means you need to have a point of view. If the member is a climate change denier, you need to make that member aware of the prevailing scientific consensus. But it also means that you realize you're taking the member somewhere—from what he or she knows currently to a new state of knowledge. The first part, point of view, we'll explore in much greater depth when talking about how librarians improve society in chapter 7. The second part, changing states of knowledge—or what we'll simply call "learning"—that's what we'll explore now.

Learning through Conversation

As a librarian, you are an educator. You're not in the information business because we don't really know what information is. You're not in the book business because people in the book business don't wrap books in durable plastic and stick bar codes on them. You're in the knowledge creation business. You're in the learning business. Whether you spend your time gathering and organizing resources, answering questions online, or standing in front of classes, you're all about learning.

People learn by reading. People learn by doing. People learn in groups and alone. People learn, it seems, in a myriad of ways. Except that they don't. People learn from *conversations*.

Although this was posited by a fellow by the name of Gordon Pask in his *Conversation Theory*,[5] the idea pervades learning theories from those of cognitive psychology to those of pedagogy and of social interactions. In fact, so many people have come to the conclusion that learning takes place in conversation they've created an overarching term: "dialectic theories."[6]

The basics go like this. You understand the world in a certain way. We'll call that your "current state of knowledge." When you encounter new ideas, you process them, and change that current state of knowledge into a new state of knowledge. We call that change "learning." I know this seems really elementary, but it gets very interesting very quickly.

Now this new state of knowledge may be radically different from your previous state (a Eureka moment), or it may be different in the most trivial way. But, just to be clear, *any* change in that state of knowledge is learning. Furthermore, learning is not just an accumulation of facts, but a network of beliefs and understandings. Is 68° warm or cool? Are the Bears a better football team than the Patriots? What's the best variety of apples? The process of learning, however, remains the same. Let's break this process down into specific ideas because each idea helps define the work of librarians.

Conversants

At first blush, learning through conversation makes intuitive sense. You learn from talking with teachers and experts. However, you are probably thinking that you learn a lot of things through activities other than conversation. Reading, for example. Except that reading *is* a conversation. It's just a conversation with yourself. In learning theory, we refer to this as "metacognition." This is very important because when you read, you're not having a conversation with the book or screen, nor are you talking with the author (even if that author's still alive). You're talking with *yourself*. Your reading can confuse or enlighten you, but, either way, it changes you—you are learning. What's more, you learn from conversations about fiction and nonfiction alike: opinions, beliefs, facts, laws, songs, art—all generate conversations and learning.

The Nigerian writer Chimamanda Adichie stresses the importance of breaking down stereotypes and prejudices of foreign cultures through literature.[7] She contends that many in Western cultures see places like Africa in shallow, two-dimensional terms because they have so few narratives about them in their media. She talks about how many in the West see African countries like Nigeria simply as places of poverty, or sickness, or civil strife because those are the only stories they encounter, not the stories about growing up in Nigeria, or about love and ambition there. Only by opening ourselves up to conversations beyond event-driven news can we come to truly empathize with a people.

We need to have rich and deep conversations with ourselves on a wide range of topics, from technology, to history, to science fiction, to romance, so that our state of knowledge is rich and varied. What's more, we need to not limit our knowledge to things that are easily put into words. We learn from aesthetic experiences—from a painting or a song that moves us, for example. Thus learning as mediated by librarians should not be limited to purely utilitarian facts and figures.

Of course we also converse with people. Most of these interpersonal conversations come from those close to use—friends and family. It is why our politics start out looking like those of our parents, and why often time our Facebook feeds are filled with confirming evidence of our worldview—because we filter out ideas and conversations we don't agree with.

Trust Me, I'm a Librarian

The concepts of conversation and conversants are crucial to the work of librarians because we want to be included in our community members' conversations, which means we need to be not just accessible but also credible. Credibility is one of the key assets of librarians. The good news is that, just by including yourself in the ranks of librarians, you start with the benefit of the doubt—people tend to trust librarians. That said, credibility is a fickle thing and easily lost.

Previous approaches to credibility saw it as an attribute of a channel or source. Thus TV might be seen as more credible than the Internet, and the president of the United States, as credible because of his position. Yet today we see credibility as something much more nuanced, as an aspect invested in a channel or person by the learner. For example, there are plenty of people who distrust authority in all its forms and who therefore find the president of the United States *less* credible because of his position. Credibility is not some inherent attribute of a person, resource, or position; it is something we learn as part of our knowledge, and that knowledge can change.

One of the clearest examples of this was seen in the aftermath of Hurricane Katrina in New Orleans. Many people displaced by the flooding that ravaged the city turned to official agencies for help, only to receive instructions that were conflicting or downright wrong. The agencies lost credibility in the eyes of the citizens, who turned to online forums, many offered by the local newspaper, to find the answers themselves. What emerged were sources seen as credible not because of their official titles, but because the answers they gave worked. "Authority" was replaced by "reliability."

This reliability model of credibility has extended to almost all aspects of our life. Rather than listening to the weather report on the evening news, we watch the real-time radar to plan our day. Rather than simply following the directives of our doctors, we independently read up on medication and side effects on websites like WebMD and Medline. In a world of easily accessed digital resources, we have moved from accepting someone's authority based on position, to disputing that authority and looking elsewhere for credible, reliable guidance.

In this world of credibility by reliability, librarians are stars. That is because librarians provide services in a transparent, principled, and consistent fashion. Note, they do so with consistency in principles and intent, rather than in form and function, as libraries do in their role as institutions, discussed in later chapters.

I can't stress it enough: we must be credible if we are to fulfill our mission as librarians. If our communities don't trust us, we can't help them improve. That trust must be earned over time, however, and granted to us by our communities. Trust comes from a mutal respect, not from a disputable neutrality that refuses to take stands. In the language of learning, we must be credible conversants. And what, as conversants, are we doing in our conversations with community members? We're exchanging language.

Language

In order for learning to take place, there has to be some sort of effort. After all, you don't learn through osmosis. You can't simply surround yourself with books and expect to learn. If this worked, I wouldn't have failed French in high school. So, what are all these conversants doing? The first thing they are doing is exchanging *language*.

Once again, my focus here is on spoken and written language, but this does not exclude the language of dance or sound or body language for that matter. It's just that librarians have traditionally focused on language that can be stored.

So what kind of language are the conversants sharing? It comes down to two basic types: "L_0" and "L_1." L_0 is language where at least one of the conversants has little knowledge of the topic being discussed. It tends to be directional and is used mostly to negotiate meanings and terms at a very simple level, to set the stage for deeper, more engaged conversations. We use L_0 a lot in our life for simple directions, introducing ourselves to strangers, and so on, and there's great power in this level of language. L_1 language, on the other hand, is where both conversants have a higher understanding of the topic being discussed and where real learning (knowledge creation) occurs; it is used to negotiate agreements.

Take the conversations that might follow if one conversant asks the other: "How do I get to Carnegie Hall?" If the asker is a grade-schooler from Wisconsin who's come to New York City for the first time, and the person asked a subway token booth clerk at Grand Central Station, the answer will likely be something like "You take the uptown Lexington Avenue Express to the 59th Street stop, then transfer to the downtown Broadway Express …" They're using L_0 language. But if the asker is a grad student wearing an NYU sweatshirt and the person asked is a homegrown newsstand owner, the answer might well be "Practice, practice, practice!" Both conversants might chuckle (or groan) at the old joke and swap guesses as to whether it really was Jack Benny who told it first. They're using L_1 language.[8]

One of the best L_0 interfaces on the web is Google. If you type in "How do you get to Carnegie Hall?" it will spit out "About 11,300,000 results" in "0.78 seconds." The first result is most likely a map of New York City. Then you start seeing results on the old joke, including attribution to Jack Benny, even though the first results clearly state it wasn't Jack Benny who came up with the joke. What Google is doing is trying to add some background facets about your context into the query you gave it. It's trying to turn your L_0 query into an L_1 conversation. So it adds things like your location, previous search results, and YouTube videos you watched to try and dig deeper than "how + to + get + to + Carnegie + Hall." You see, L_1 language is where you begin to talk about substance. As people become more knowledgeable about a topic, they represent that deeper knowledge in the terms they use. So as an information scientist, for example, I can talk about "relevance" to grad students or to other information scientists and know that the term will be associated with a whole history of inquiry, experimentation, and publications in the information retrieval literature.

You do this, too. At your work, in college, or simply by living where you do. Here are two quick examples. Each time I give you a word, write down the first thing that comes to mind.

Light

Okay, did you write "illumination" or perhaps "not heavy"? How about "to set on fire," as in light a candle? But if you're trying to watch your weight, you most likely wrote "low in calories." Next word.

Formula

Did you write "mathematical expression?" Probably, if you've read this chapter straight through. How about "chemical recipe," like the formula for gunpowder? If you're a new mother or father (or aunt, or grandparent), you most likely wrote "something you feed to babies."

You see language, like knowledge itself, is a set of relationships. Some relationships we use all the time and are reinforced (you use "turn on the lights" more than "light the house on fire"). Other meanings are there, but because we don't use them all the time they become unexpected. You knew formula was given to babies, but you probably smiled a little when I mentioned it to you not because it was new information, but because it was an unexpected pairing. This varied connected concepts with words is the basis of a huge range of comedy—the true, but unexpected punch line ... how do you get to Carnegie Hall? Practice.

We could keep going, but I have to take this opportunity to jump ahead to talking about libraries for a moment. If you do this same sort of experiment with the general public and ask them to give you one word to describe a library, the most likely answer you will get back is "book" or "books." Many have taken this as our members wanting books from their libraries. But just as with light and formula, there is attached to this word a huge network of possible meanings. Is a book a surrogate for something I read, or learning, or stories, or what?

Bottom line: as librarians, we must see language as something more complex than a collection of words or terms. People and groups use special language to speed communication, to exclude people from conversations, and for a whole host of other reasons. If we're going to help our community members learn, we must be able to communicate with them in their language whenever possible or at least to negotiate a new language for our exchanges. We can't simply take a question and type it into Google. And we can't build systems that do that either.

Why does Google do a better job with simple searches than library catalogs? Because Google seeks to see how terms are connected to a broad range of resources, whereas library catalogs seek to match them to an L_1 system that only librarians truly understand. Where Google took the words "how + to + get + to + Carnegie + Hall" and found matches in maps, archives, and discussion groups, library catalogs try to find matches in books as classified by the Dewey Decimal System or by the Library of Congress (or another system).

Librarians for centuries have been attempting to reduce the complexity of language to an efficient, specialized "classification system." We felt that if we could all agree on one means of labeling a thing, then we could more easily find that thing. It is the same logic that, if we all just spoke one language, like English, all misunderstandings would go away. We see how well this has worked when US diplomats speak to the people of England, and Australia, and the world's largest pool of English speakers, China.

To be fair, these specialized language systems have worked exceptionally well, particularly in a world of physical objects and limited time and capacity. But it has become increasingly clear that, in reducing complexity, we have also reduced understanding and nuance by assuming that everyone's language and meaning were the same.

This idea in language and in science is called reductionism. Reductionism is the belief that if you take anything complex and break it into its component parts, and break those down again and again until you understand the smaller parts, you can understand the whole. Take a car engine apart; understand the parts, and you can build a new engine. Except with language, and most human endeavors, this approach doesn't work.

Take *My Two Super Dads*,[9] a storybook about a girl who has two gay fathers. If you're organizing a collection of materials, where do you slot this one in? In fiction (the intent of the author)? Gender studies? In political works? Family studies, knowing that what constitutes a family is not universal? Your job as a librarian, as a professional, is not simply to apply existing tools like classification systems in some seemingly objective way. It is to understand the complexity of thought in your community, and to respond as best you can to match that complexity as you engage with community members. And that leads us to what all these exchanges of language are about in the first place: seeking agreements.

Agreements

Let's start with something no one can deny: the world is round. Except, of course, that people *can* deny it. Even setting aside the "flat-earthers" (yes, they still exist), and confining ourselves to the scientific or rational world of librarianship, there are still people who can deny the Earth is round. Because, as carefully measured and remeasured, it really *isn't* round, or at least not perfectly round. It's what's called an "oblate spheroid," flatter at its poles and fatter round its middle. As physicists see it, the Earth also exists in four space-time dimensions, so its shape is always changing. Or, as some people think, the Earth may not exist at all in the normal sense of the word, much less be round, but be a holographic projection of an underlying reality. That last view is not from *The Matrix*, by the way, but from an actual scientific paper.[10]

Now, once again, I can hear you say, "Thou doth protest too much." The views I've just listed are really just refinements (well, all but the last one) of something we can all agree on. And there's that word: "agree." Remember when I said that knowledge is a set of interrelated agreements? Well, it's time to talk about those agreements. That the Earth is round is not a fact; it's an agreement put into words. Part of that agreement limits what you're talking about. You may be happier with simply saying, "Generally, the Earth can be considered round," but that's wordy, so you just shorten it. We've already done the same with $1 + 1 = 2$ because what that really says is "The sum of 1 and 1 is 2 in base 10." We hold agreements on all sorts of things, not just facts. Blue skies are nice, that dog is cute, and so on. We come up with these agreements through conversations where the conversants are exchanging language.

This work itself is an example of trying to guide internal conversations to arrive at certain agreements about the field of librarianship. To be clear, it's trying to guide your internal conversation, not with the book, or myself as an author, but with yourself as learner.

Why does this matter to you as a librarian? Well, remember all those times I said you can't simply respond to a community member's request or question by providing answers or resources? That you had to respond by understanding the context of that member? What you're trying to do is come up with agreements.

"You say you want information on climate change. Would you prefer scholarly articles or things from the popular press? Although there's a scientific consensus on the reality of human-caused climate change, would you also like to see minority dissenting views?" Note, by the way, that the language you're using ("minority views") is already exposing preexisting agreements you hold.

Note, also, that these agreements can be made manifest in ways other than the language we use. Dewey placing books on cooking in with books on business, for example. Or even in how we organize physical spaces. I've walked into school libraries filled with stacks and very few desks, where the librarian and the community that librarian serves have agreed that the best use of the space was to house materials. On the other hand, I've also walked into school libraries with a few low shelves and a large number of round tables, where they've agreed that the best use of the space was group work. Of course, I'm assuming this was an agreement with the community and not just a librarian making their own agreements physical.

Remember our word game with "light" and "formula"? Each word has a network of agreed-upon meanings. Some of these networks are quite small. If I say "granite," it's pretty certain you'll think of a type of rock (or counter tops if you're in the real estate business). As we've seen, however, terms like "library" and "radical" can have a huge network of agreed-upon meanings.

So, as librarians, we seek first to understand the agreements in place with those we serve, then add to or help change those associated agreements. But here's the key: we must start with where people are now. If incoming freshmen believe the best sources for a research paper need no documentation, simply telling them they're wrong and showing them the peer-reviewed literature to that effect won't work. You must build from what they do now (a reflection of what they believe) and help move them to where you want them to be. Also, understand that both the starting and ending points are knowledge, as defined here, because both will affect their behavior.

Memory

So now you're done, right? Your community members have learned (and, most likely, so have you). You've created knowledge. Except for one thing. If you don't remember your agreements, there's no learning. The fourth vital component of knowledge creation (with conversants, language, and agreements) is *memory*. Without memory, we'd have to constantly renegotiate agreements and discover everything anew.

Now you might think that memory is a simple thing: an account of agreements, events, and such over time. But that's not how memory works. For example, as we've established, at some point in your life you learned $1 + 1 = 2$. But you probably don't remember exactly when unless something very significant also happened at that time. Memory is not like a computer with inputs and outputs. It's a complex web. Many, many agreements go into our knowledge, yet their exact origins disappear in what psychologists call "source amnesia."[11] For a moment of agreement to stand out, it must have lots of meaning and lots of connections, mostly emotional. Even then, there's a good chance that our memory of an event is also colored by those meanings and connections.

Take a significant moment in time from your life. Your wedding, the birth of your first child, your first kiss. Now picture it clearly in your mind. What color socks were you wearing? Unless socks were part of your memory (my aunt had to bring me black socks on my wedding day because I forgot to pack them), you won't remember what color they were. Memory is a network of agreements over time. Parts of that network are reinforced and kept, parts are not and lost, and most are reinterpreted in the light of new knowledge.

Memory is also important because it is relational. If you're like most people, you had a hard time in history memorizing who was president when, and who conquered whom when. This is the reason so few historians teach history that way. Dates matter, but the themes and ideas that we learn from moments in the past are much more powerful. Not only that, but history is rarely seen as simply a linear progression of events. History scholars don't simply recount events in order, they seek out themes and influences to illuminate the past in light of the present.

Take something like Columbus discovering America in 1492. Except that he didn't. There were plenty of native peoples already living in the "New" World. A way of looking at Columbus—sailing the ocean blue in 1492—is being replaced, or at least augmented in schools and society, with a new view—the impact of that "discovery" on native populations. So did history change? No, but how we interpret it, and our perspectives and language did.

What does this mean to you as a librarian? Well, not every community you'll engage with is going to have the same memory of events. For example, the city of Syracuse, where I live, has many issues commonly associated with urban centers in the United States; poverty, segregation, unemployment, and, youth violence. It seems like the community goes through cycles, with sudden upsurges of street violence and gang activity. Almost like clockwork, the police, the mayor, and community leaders sound the alarm and begin a series of town forums and launch new initiatives to curb youth violence. Is there a way that librarians could

1. jump-start the process of addressing youth violence by taking what worked the last time it occurred and highlighting that for civic officials, or, preferably,

2. keep the memory alive and present to prevent falling back into the conditions that lead to the violence in the first place?

Making best use of the relational nature of memory needs to be among the librarians' tools in engaging with their communities. Can public librarians embed the history of their communities into their buildings, as they've done with the Memorial Room at the Fairfield Public Library in Connecticut? There the whole room is covered with murals and plaques that re-create the history of the town and memorialize soldiers from Fairfield who lost their lives. When members of the library board or civic groups meet in this room, they can feel how their actions connect to and build on the actions of those who've gone before them. The Vatican Library takes this one step further. On its ceilings above the scholars working below are fifteenth-century frescoes that tell the story of book making from the manufacture of paper to printing to selling to education to the value of reading for pleasure.

School librarians can provide more than books to students for history projects. They can team with teachers to organize field trips to local historical sites, and they can even host historical reenactments. Across the globe, librarians work with historians, archivists, and preservationists not simply to preserve the past, but also to make it accessible and relevant to their members today, by compiling photo archives accessible not just by date, but by theme (poverty, civil rights, urban violence).

Bottom line: as librarians, we can act to represent and preserve agreements over time within our communities. In doing so, we can foster knowledge creation, enable new understandings of the past, and speed discovery of new opportunities.

The Practicalities of Being in the Conversation Business

As we'll see throughout the rest of this guide, knowledge creation through conversation will shape everything librarians do. For example, why should you as a librarian (we'll ask this question again for libraries) build a collection? If you start with a loose, commonsense definition of "librarian"— "someone who works in a library"—the answer would be, "Because libraries have collections." This tautology—librarians build collections because libraries have collections— gives us no sense of why. With our view of knowledge creation, however, librarians can build collections to fuel a learning process: either an internal conversation of a community member or a conversation among many members. Furthermore, collections can document agreements in language that can be understood by a community and provide an accurate memory of these agreements over time. On the other hand, there is nothing in our view of knowledge creation that *requires* a collection. Building a collection is only appropriate for some communities, not an inherent part of librarianship.

We also see that *where* a conversation occurs is also important. This is not just a question of building spaces and whether those spaces should be quiet or not. Librarians should go to where the conversations are occurring. With the advent of increasingly connected and mobile technologies, this is easier and easier. Librarians can do their work on subways and in homes, in business meetings, Facebook Groups, and even deep in the forests of Colombia.[12]

By seeing learning as conversations not confined by a space or a time, and librarianship as independent of the buildings and institutions called "libraries," we can expand our mission of improving society further than ever before. There are, of course, many reasons to build libraries, something we'll talk about later on. But these reasons are no longer the bounds of librarianship and the knowledge creation we facilitate. They are simply hubs and tools in our pursuit of a better tomorrow.

5 Facilitation

Core Chapter Concept: Librarians facilitate knowledge creation through access, knowledge, environment, and motivation.

Let's take stock. Where are we? Librarians are professionals on a mission to improve society through facilitating knowledge creation in our communities. We do this in libraries and in many other contexts. The way we view knowledge, as a set of related agreements arrived at through internal and external conversations, shapes everything we do. Now it's time to look at that shaping in action. What do librarians do? We facilitate.

You may ask, with all this discussion of learning and knowledge, why not just say that librarians teach? The answer to that question comes directly from chapter 4, on knowledge creation. To learn is an active choice by the learner, who must choose to be a conversant and who must participate in the dialogue. Bottom line: you can't teach an unwilling pupil.

As a librarian, indeed as a human being, I can't teach you anything if you choose not to learn. So what librarians do is to create the conditions for people to learn. They can do this directly (actively working with members) or indirectly (assembling a collection of materials for members to explore in their conversations). Either way, along with our mission and values, our means of facilitation, founded on our understanding of knowledge creation, uniquely define us as librarians.

So how can librarians create conditions for learning, that is, facilitate knowledge creation? In four ways. We can

- provide *access* to conversations and materials to enrich conversations;
- enhance *knowledge* creation through direct instruction;
- provide an *environment* conducive to learning; and
- provide or build upon the *motivation* of our members or communities.

All four of these ways are necessary for learning. Let's break each of them down, starting with the means that most librarians think they do a good job with, even when they often do only half the job.

Access

Librarians can provide access to knowledge and materials that inspire and enhance learning conversations. Many interpret this as organizing collections of artifacts like books and digital resources. Although that might be part of what we do, there are plenty of librarians who do their work with *no* collections at all, and, besides, we do *much* more than simply collect resources (books, magazines, journals), whose value comes not from their aggregation, but from how they support knowledge creation in our communities.

Let's start with the "materials that can inspire and enhance learning conversations" because that's where many librarians get stuck. "Inspiring materials" include far more than books or written materials. Because paintings can also inspire, some librarians build collections of art if that's appropriate for their communities. Seeking to support architects and interior designers, librarians in New York City created a library of building materials. In Italy, the librarians of a library for the transportation industry and scholars put together a collection of actual trains—locomotives, passenger and freight cars, everything. In Illinois, youth services librarians collect robotics kits, try them out, and then blog about what works and what doesn't for their young members, parents, and other librarians. Those kits and the blog postings are their collections.[1]

But the key here is that librarians facilitate knowledge creation by providing access to *conversations* and materials. In the 1980s, Joan Bechtel talked about how academic librarians should be teaching students that the scholarly literature is in fact a scholarly discourse—a conversation.[2] Indeed, the materials students and scholars were accessing, from journal papers to conference presentations to books, were best understood as the artifacts of ongoing dialogue on the nature of a field.

Because knowledge is uniquely human, one of the fundamental means that librarians use to facilitate knowledge creation is connecting people around common activities or interests. We can do this by curating spaces that allow people to interact in social ways or by organizing intensive work groups. We can also connect our members with experts who have answers to their questions.

But here's how our view of access and librarianship is changing fundamentally. Rather than simply bringing the world to our members, as librarians have been doing for centuries, we must now look at how we can establish *two-way* ongoing conversations between the world and our community members—by also bringing our members' expertise and knowledge to the rest of the world.

Imagine planning a trip, say, from your home in Syracuse to Wellington, New Zealand. You'd think nothing of going to your library in Syracuse to get information on New Zealand. But why couldn't you go to the Wellington City Library to learn about that city? Not physically, but virtually. Imagine if the librarians there made it possible for local musicians, restaurateurs, and historians to share their music, views, and experience with the outside world by hosting podcasts, recordings, and videos—by arranging to give outside members a virtual guided tour of downtown Wellington.

Bottom line: for librarians, access must be a two-way proposition. Librarians provide access to knowledge external to a community, and expertise of the community externally (and to itself as we will see). Librarians embedded in research teams don't just spend time running down articles, they blog about research results and optimize discoverability of their findings. School librarians don't just bring authors into the library; they post the illustrations of their students and create science fair teams linked across continents. Librarians must stop leading with their backs to their communities assuming that the knowledge people seek resides outside of the boundaries of the community served. Librarians are platforms and publishers of the community as much as (and in the future more so than) consumers of publications.

Knowledge

Remember that I said you can't teach an unwilling pupil? Well, sometimes the will is there, but the means are not. Take, as an example, a doctoral student (let's call her "Joanne") doing dissertation research on the topic of the role of women in ancient Persian society. As a librarian, you may be able to identify numerous resources and experts on the topic. However, if almost all of these require that Joanne have a working understanding of ancient and modern Persian, and she speaks only English, then, absent additional help, no significant learning can occur. In this case, in addition to access, the librarian must help the member build *knowledge* about the conversations she needs to enter into. This could be anything from referring Joanne to translation services to showing her where she can receive the language training she needs.

A standing set of enabling knowledge is a "curriculum." Most librarians build and support curricula around the concept of information literacy. Be it in primary school, university, a public library workshop, or a course in professional development training for those in business, librarians foster a set of skills to quickly identify needed knowledge, access that knowledge (or resources to prompt knowledge creation), evaluate the sources of knowledge, synthesize new knowledge into existing understandings (the act of knowledge creation), and, finally, evaluate the whole process.

There are many models of information literacy—the one I briefly outlined is a rough approximation of "the Big6" model developed by Mike Eisenberg and Bob Berkowitz—"a six-stage model to help anyone solve problems or make decisions by using information."[3] What they all share, however, is an expanded idea of literacy.

Many people limit literacy and literacy skills to reading. Librarians, so goes their thinking, teach reading skills and foster literacy (and a love of reading). Except, of course, that they don't, or at least not all of them. There are plenty of librarians who work in settings and communities where literacy in its most basic sense is simply assumed. Medical librarians don't spend a lot of time working with doctors on their basic reading skills. But they do spend a lot of time worrying about literacy in its extended or larger senses.

You'll recall that in chapter 4, on knowledge creation, I talked about how knowledge is relational. We hold agreements not as discrete sets of facts, but as intricate networks of understandings. Literacy is the ability to find and use these relationships in the knowledge of others in the world we encounter. To be literate in reading means you can recognize not only the letters and words but also the patterns of language. As their literacy skills expand, readers can become writers and can analyze texts in great depth. Mathematical literacy starts with simple number manipulation, but can eventually be expressed as a sort of symphony of concepts and procedures that we hope may unlock a unifying theory of the very universe.

From media literacy, to financial literacy, to cultural literacy, to computer literacy, librarians understand that, to empower their members, they must help them identify and capitalize on patterns of knowledge in a given area.

Think about how much of college curricula and modes of instruction is based on identifying and utilizing patterns. The Socratic method is alive and well, at least in academe. As you progress through formal education, what knowledge is all about shifts ever more rapidly from memorized facts and figures to critical thinking and analysis. This was once put beautifully by a graduate student of mine:

When I was an undergraduate, if I asked a question, the professor would give me an answer. When I was a master's student, the professor would respond with "What a great question ... how will *you* answer it?" And, finally, when I was a doctoral student, the professor and I would spend all day trying to refine the question to see if it was in fact good.

Knowledge as represented and disseminated by librarians is much more about an ability to learn in an ongoing way than about gathering documents together. The reference interview is not a series of questions and answers meant to arrive at an answer; it is in fact an intensive and hyper-focused course on a topic of a member's choosing. As librarians, we pick books or cite articles or acquire resources not because of what they are in themselves, but because of how they may benefit our communities' learning.

Environment

Okay, let's revisit our doctoral student Joanne looking for information on the role of women in ancient Persia. Let's say she has access to experts and ongoing venues of dialogue and resources relevant to her topic. Let's go further and say, with the aid of a librarian, Joanne has actually gained a working knowledge of ancient and modern Persian (perhaps by the librarian connecting her to a language center on campus). So that she's all set to begin a conversation with scholars who communicate primarily in Persian, and who all happen to work in Iran for the purposes of this example. If Joanne is from the United States (and even if she isn't), this might suddenly create challenges that have nothing to do with the Persian language or even with her topic, at least not directly. That Joanne will be dealing with scholars in Iran, a country the U.S. State Department describes as an "active state sponsor of terrorism," might bring her under government scrutiny, for example.

This may seem like an extreme example, but there are a huge number of cases where, to learn something, a community member (scholar, student, housewife, businessperson) has to venture into some areas that will make others uncomfortable. The third means of facilitation used by librarians in knowledge creation is to provide an *environment* conducive to learning, where members feel safe—sometimes providing physical safety, but always providing intellectual safety.

We will come back to the idea of physical safety when we talk about libraries and organizations, but the main point here is that, if members lack a sense of physical safety, they are greatly impaired in their ability (and certainly their desire) to learn. We can foster a sense of safety by arranging to work with our members in safe places we provide (not only libraries), or by going to places where the members already feel safe, at home or at the office, for example. As librarians, we need to consider, how safe do our members feel when they have to approach one of us sitting behind an imposing elevated reference desk? Do they feel safe from embarrassment in public situations? How about if they have to use the latest technology, say, for video conferencing?

Still, for now, let's focus on intellectual safety. How do we provide a safe intellectual environment for our community members? Some of the ways come from the long-standing values of our profession. For example, in providing access to experts and materials that span the gambit of sources from the approved to the banned, we can guarantee our members' privacy by not sharing their inquiries or conversations unless they give us explicit permission to do so.

In facilitating conversations, librarians can also provide safe spaces where people with different viewpoints and different backgrounds can talk. For example, all across the globe, librarians have built "Human Libraries."[4] In a Human Library, people can "check out" individuals different from them, lawyers, or mechanics, or college professors, gays, or Muslims, or homeless people, for example to engage in conversations. By ensuring these conversations will be civil, we can provide safe spaces for them to happen.

We can also directly mediate conversations, ensuring that no one voice dominates a discussion. We need to learn effective meeting strategies and how to deal with the power relationships involved. We need to make sure that minority voices are heard. And we can enrich ongoing conversations. For example, in many colleges, librarians sit in on classes, either physically or virtually. Professors can ask for clarifications, and the librarians can provide quick answers, either in person or on their laptops.

The point is that for a conversation to occur—a necessary precondition to learning—community members must feel free to express their ideas, and they must know that their ideas will be heard. As librarians, we can set the ground rules to make this happen.

There is one last way in which librarians use environments to encourage learning. We can create spaces (virtual and real) that inspire. Although this might seem like a conversation best saved for our discussion of libraries, inspiration can come from many different kinds of environments, not just physical ones. For example, we can build websites that showcase the accomplishments of member or aspirational peers. We can highlight inspirational quotes or find images that inspire action. We can also ensure that the resources we create represent diversity in a welcoming, respectful environment. Too often the digital resources that librarians create either show a homogeneous population (only white people) or no community at all (images of empty rooms). We must make sure that these virtual environments are also representative of our members and communities and honor their expectations.

Motivation

If someone doesn't want to learn, that someone simply won't, no matter what access or knowledge you provide and no matter how welcoming and safe the environment. Learners must *want* to learn.

That doesn't mean, however, that you can't have an effect on a member's internal motivation. As a librarian, you can use external motivation to move people toward wanting to learn. As a librarian you have the ability to use extrinsic motivation to push people toward learning. At a simple level this is building yourself into larger processes. For example, after an insufficient literature review led to deaths as part of a clinical trial at Johns Hopkins the university implemented a mandatory librarian consultation process. Researchers had to work with librarians to guarantee an exhaustive search of existing research and side effects was done before clinical trials. Some university and industry projects must include consultation with librarians to ensure adequate archiving or data distribution.

We will cover more of these examples at the institutional level when we talk about libraries as institutions (marketing, integration into faculty tenure review, open access publishing, government record keeping, and such). The point is that while many librarians have depended on intrinsic motivation to bring community members to the librarian, there are many important opportunities for librarians to require their services. Once again, this does not ensure learning, but it uses incentives to increase the opportunities for engagement, conversation, and learning.

But it's important for librarians to first be aware of what might be motivating members to learn, and then to array tools and services to stimulate and support those internal motivations. This means in our interactions we need to determine the underlying drives and aspirations of our members. For example, are they looking into nutrition because they really want to lose weight? Get healthy? Feed their families better? Write term papers on the topic? Their underlying motivations shape the types and forms of answers you can provide and the time they'll need to spend to make best use of those answers.

All Together Now

As mentioned before, you need all four of these means of facilitation to ensure that learning takes place; only rarely will you use them in isolation. Let me present an example of these means in action, adapted from real life and anonymized to protect the innocent.

A law librarian sitting at her desk was approached one morning by a partner in her law firm, who said, "I've been searching for information on this expert witness, but I've found very little, and I'm due in court in two hours. Can you help me?"

The expert witnesses called by the prosecution and defense to help make their arguments in a criminal case are doctors, professors, or other professionals with a deep understanding of some topic in the case. Opposing lawyers do their best to challenge or refute the testimony of witnesses called by the other side, which often means challenging their credentials or expertise or their positions in some way. To do this, the lawyers must access the witnesses' backgrounds, records, publications, and public statements and sift through these for faults, inconsistencies, or contradictions. The partner had tried to do this for one particular expert witness but with few results.

After getting the name and title of the expert witness and the basics of the case from the partner, in a matter of minutes, the law librarian was printing out publications by and articles and other documents about the witness. With these in hand, the partner was able to find what he needed before he had to be in court.

Now we could stop the story there—Librarian saves the day! But this librarian did much more than just save the day. She began to offer regular classes in "Character Assassination 101" at her firm, where she would walk lawyers and their aides through doing online research into experts. "You can search this database ... or I could do it for you." "This is how to find an article written by an expert ... or you could have me do it."

In this example, we see all four means of facilitation in action. The law librarian provided *access* for her community members, both to resources and to one another's own tips and techniques on how to look for what they needed, which they could share in her classes. She enhanced their *knowledge* creation through direct instruction by teaching about online searching and data analysis. Her choosing the name "Character Assassination 101" for her course was partly a joke, but it was also a reflection of the culture of her law firm and helped her provide an *environment* conducive to learning. Finally, the librarian recognized and built upon the intrinsic *motivation* of the layers to perform well in their cases.

These means of facilitation can play an important role in traditional library services as well, where an "answer" to a reference question may be an expanding series of learning interactions that show members how to locate resources and expertise. It may involve broadcasting a member's question via social media. It will involve instruction—from simple show and tell to creating whole courses. It may involve protecting the privacy of members in their investigations, or the exact opposite, rewarding them by publically recognizing the learning they have achieved.

These means of facilitation can all be seen in cataloging and organizing resources. As librarians, we need to go beyond describing a text; using all of our means of facilitation, we need to relate that text to our community members and their learning. These means of facilitation also call for a radically new approach to building technology systems for our communities. No longer can we survey a set of people and resources and simply place links to these on a website or in a database. We must curate the collection, providing links that specifically serve our communities' interests and goals. We must align resources to anticipated educational outcomes in schools, colleges, and businesses. The online sites we create must provide our members with a place for conversation, not simply with access to documents and websites.

As a librarian, using your tools of facilitation, you must go deep into the needs, dreams, and aspirations of your community. Those tools, the services you provide, and the functions you perform will change as your community changes. Which is a perfect segue to rethinking the whole concept of community.

6 Participatory Systems

Core Chapter Concept: Librarians serve their communities through the participatory systems they build, some of which are libraries.

So librarians are on a mission to improve society. They do this by facilitating knowledge creation in their communities, through access, knowledge, environment, and motivation. So how exactly do they do this? They build systems. The *Oxford English Dictionary* defines "system" as "a set or assemblage of things connected, associated, or interdependent, so as to form a complex unity." Books are systems, websites are systems, story times are systems, and so are libraries.

Librarian-built systems might include web pages, or apps, or courses such as "Character Assassination 101," talked about in chapter 5. Some of these systems are highly technical in nature, such as metadata schemas and catalog software. Others are completely physical, such as how stacks are arranged for browsing printed materials. But of all the systems built by librarians, there are special ones that are so complex the entire second part of this guide is devoted to them, systems we call "libraries."

The important thing to note, however, is that, to facilitate knowledge creation in their communities, librarians must build systems that allow for learning, which is a participatory act. Because you can't teach people something unless they're willing to learn, that means they must also be willing to participate. And because people learn through conversations, the systems we build must allow for two-way conversations—they must be participatory.

Pressure for Participation

To be clear, having one person or group speak *at* another person or group is not a conversation. Take, for example, a college lecture. The central conversations occurring in the lecture hall aren't between the lecturing professor and audience members—the central conversations are *within* the individual listeners. A bad lecture is one person talking *at* audience members. A good lecture is one person prompting those members to have internal dialogues. A great lecture is an opening statement to an interactive discussion that often goes on long after the class or course is over; indeed, that may go on for a lifetime.

If you want to facilitate knowledge creation and therefore conversations, you must create opportunities for participation. Indeed, if learners are to learn, they will exert pressure to participate on any system or person seeking to help them in that endeavor.

The pressure to participate has at least five different aspects:

- the pressure to converse;
- the pressure for change;
- the pressure for social interaction;
- the pressure of limited resources; and
- the pressure of boundaries.

Let's take each of these in turn.

The Pressure to Converse

At the heart of the first aspect of the pressure to participate is the desire simply to be heard. Audience members in a lecture hall will want to ask questions. Students in a classroom will want to have their ideas at least acknowledged.

On a larger scale, imagine offering an online class to over 2,000 participants. Some of them will want to talk on hierarchical discussion boards; others will prefer to speak to one another in real time—or via social media. In any case, unless they can be heard, indeed, unless they can converse, many participants will refuse to use the tools you provide. They'll make their own tools, or simply leave the class.

We see in system after system that when the ability to provide feedback or to converse with others members is withheld, people will build their own mechanisms. For college students frustrated by the narrowness of class evaluations there is RateMyProfessor.com. When Walmart didn't respond to criticism by their customers, they went out and built WalmartSucks.org. In fact there is an entire top level domain of the Internet, .sucks, dedicated to just such complaint sites.

This pressure to converse doesn't mean people won't use broadcast systems, or that putting up a comment form is sufficient. Community members want a conversation, not just a place to rant or a suggestion drop box. They need to see that you are listening to the feedback. They need to converse with other community members.

The Pressure for Change

When you build a system for a group of your community members, allow them to be part of the design process. Build in the ability for them to alter and customize the system after the fact. This is not just about seeing what your members do and trying to match that with an interface—it's about allowing your members to directly alter the functioning and structure of the system to meet their needs.

Here's a story to illustrate this point. A group of librarians held a "bristle bots" workshop for eight- to ten-year-olds, a pretty common activity to introduce kids to the idea of making things. A bristle bot is nothing more than the head of a toothbrush glued to a pager motor. When you connect the motor to a battery, the bristles of the brush head vibrate and move around. About eight children showed up for the workshop. They watched as the three librarians cut off toothbrush heads, glued them to pager motors, and then connected the motors to batteries. The bots vibrated furiously—for about five seconds, then died. The librarians gave out new batteries. Same thing. It turns out they had bought the wrong kind of batteries, and the motors sucked them dry in seconds.

Quickly huddling in a corner, the librarians began frantic conversations as to where to get the right kind of batteries, who would get them, and whether they would need a purchase order. In the meantime, the kids looked around, found duct tape and some AA batteries and discovered they could build not only bristle bots, but also whole fleets of bristle destroyers, bristle hot tanks, and such. In a few minutes, the librarians noticed that, while they were worrying about how to get the right kind of batteries, the kids were busy learning without them—by doing—which was the whole point of the workshop. It was a revelatory moment for the librarians, and for me. By allowing the learners to participate, and own the activity, what could have been a disaster of disappointed kids and dead batteries became a roaring success—with the librarians in the room being the main learners. If you had asked the kids at the beginning of the workshop how it should have been run, they probably wouldn't have come up with the idea of duct tape and AA batteries. In fact, there's an excellent chance they wouldn't even have understood the question. One of the hardest parts of librarians building their work around learning and participation is that, in many cases, even though people know they want a system to change to meet their individual needs, they can't articulate what that change is.

If, as is more than likely, the system you develop is for more than a single individual, there are often competing pressures for change. The pressure to act is real, a desire for change is real, but the actual needed change is unknown, which can lead to frustration and discontent if it's not addressed.

But how to address it? For a long time, the method of addressing pressure for change was to minimize the need for change in the first place (however circular the logic of that is). The idea was through extensive research and development of "user requirements," you could build a system that met the needs of a community from the start. Through focus groups, surveys, and other methods, you could identify a community need, and build a system that would meet that need, or at least meet it for the majority of users.

Note here the term "users" versus "members" or "community members." It's not accidental: in this methodology, community members are users of a system that can be modified very little if at all after it's been built.

Want an example of a user-based system? The iPhone. No, not the iPhone you may have in your pocket or the one you can buy today. I'm talking about the original 1.0 version. It was a striking piece of technology when introduced. It brought the web, e-mail, and a phone literally to your fingertips. It was designed with thousands of hours of testing and development, and it was easy to use—but not to modify.

Many forget in these days of app stores that the apps available on the iPhone consisted solely of the ones that Apple thought you should have. No Angry Birds, no movie editing, no "app for that" tag line. And let's be clear—people loved it. It was a huge hit, but as with all systems that people use to learn and make their way through their days, pressure built for more options. People wanted to go beyond what Apple thought was needed and add their own capabilities. That pressure overcame the culture of Apple to meticulously design every aspect of the user experience. What started out as a telecommunications experience designed by the system designer (albeit with lots of initial input from user testing) became a platform for individuals to create their own connected mobile experience.

For some of you, the iPhone (or more generally smartphone) may be a texting platform with some e-mail. For others, it may be a gaming platform with a little phone calling on the side. Want to see what a difference a participatory system makes? Grab someone else's smartphone and try and figure out where that someone put something. Our phones now look much more like us. Where once we were the users of phones, now we're the orchestrators of them.

So today the systems that librarians build are about base functionality with a lot of room for ongoing changes. Indeed, if you don't build systems that change and allow community members to guide their evolution, you're doomed to having constantly to revise and renew them, and you still risk alienating your community members.

The Pressure for Social Interaction

A group of researchers monitored how undergraduates used online databases of scholarly articles. The students consistently told the researchers they found the database systems "quiet." Students were used to online systems that allowed for social interactions; they missed their peers telling them, "Here's a good article" or "Don't waste your time on this." They were used to finding resources through friends' suggestions or having a website reviewed by their community.

The database example is by no means a new phenomenon. As Clay Shirky says: "Human beings are social creatures—not occasionally or by accident but always."[1] College students have long looked for used copies of textbooks that already had good highlighting or margin notes. Information scientists have long found the first resource used in information seeking to be friends and family. In the days before online databases, one study found that the sources most cited in research papers were sources in a scholar's office, with those in the same building a distant second; materials that had to be requested through some sort of loan service were barely mentioned.

The systems that you build as a librarian must take into account this social nature. This does *not* mean every library system has to have "likes" and "friends" or the trappings put into popular culture by Facebook. It does mean that the systems need to take into account members' connections to their communities. Librarian Eli Neiburger of Ann Arbor, Michigan, talks about trying to get more teens into the library. Eli's response (one of many) to the many teens who didn't want to go to the library for fear they would lose status in the eyes of their friends was to put together a video game tournament that not only built on the gaming interest of teens, but included an element of competition. When he did, teens responded enthusiastically; indeed, they would drag their friends to the library to show off their prowess at games and their rankings.[2] The social nature of the system fit the social nature of the community.

The Pressure of Limited Resources

Let me reemphasize that when I use the terms "community" or "community members," I'm not limiting them to people who live in a given town, city, or region. A college is a community of scholars, students, and staff, a school is a community of students, teachers, and administrators, and a law firm is a community of lawyers and paralegals—wherever they may live. A community is a set of people who share at least one common known variable and a set of resources related to that variable or those variables. All of these communities have members seeking to learn and most often seeking a way to distribute scarce resources.

Let's pick up on that last point for a bit. By and large most librarians see their communities as a set of positive decisions. In other words, people chose to live or work at a place. People choose to come into the library. People chose the "variables" they align to. Except, of course, that they don't, at least not always, and maybe even not all that often. Few would choose to live in poverty. Few would choose to be part of a community of cancer patients. People have jobs they hate to allow them to do things they love. So being in a community is not always a matter of choice.

What's more, staying in a community takes more decisions than just joining one. If you live in a city you must choose your town officials. In businesses, where money is limited and time often at a premium, you must choose how much to spend of both on what. To preserve its well-being, a community must prioritize needs and allocate scarce resources. To maintain its status, while meeting its expenses, a university must set tuition rates and faculty salaries—all within the limits of available funding.

Why this trip through scarcity? It serves to remind you that all systems you build have a cost—a cost to both providers and recipients. That cost may be your time, or the cost of your time to your parent institution. It may also be an "opportunity cost": if you build this system, then you can't also build a different one. Offering a children's story time during the day may prevent you from offering a computer literacy course for seniors. Likewise, participating in a story time may cost a parent and children the opportunity of attending another function. This means you're always attempting to optimize the cost-benefit ratio of a system—balancing how much it costs with how much it benefits your community. Understanding this cost-benefit tension is one of the most important things you can learn as a librarian (or, really, as any system builder).

Some librarians think that Internet services like Google and Wikipedia make people lazy. They argue that people, be they students, faculty members, businesspersons, doctors, lawyers, whoever, could get much better information from systems like peer-reviewed article databases. Because Google and Wikipedia are so easy to use, however, people take the lazy way out and settle for "good enough," or at least that's how the argument goes. Well, wouldn't you? The answer, it turns out, is yes, you would; and finding out *why* you would won Herbert Simon a Nobel Prize in Economics. He called what almost of us do "satisficing."[3]

According to Simon, when we use a system (to seek out information, say), we're constantly trying to satisfice—to get the maximum benefit for the minimum cost. So if students can get As on their papers by searching Google rather than having to learn how to use complex databases, they will—and they should. The problem is, the students don't know ahead of time whether they'll get those As. They're making the best decisions they can with limited information. Students do it, businesses do it, governments do it. If those students end up getting Cs or worse on their papers, guess what? Next time (assuming they could attribute the low grades to their searching strategy), they would use a different strategy, or would exert more effort to raise their grades.

The trick to building systems that get used (classes that get attended, software that gets implemented, databases that get searched) is convincing people that you provide the greatest benefit for the least effort. Don't get me wrong, that "least effort" might still be quite a lot. Why do parents take their children to story time rather than sit them down in front of the TV? Because they must feel it provides their children (and maybe themselves as well) a better (more educational, more social, more meaningful) experience than watching TV. A lot of these calculations come down to choosing a more participatory experience.

The Pressure of Boundaries

As system builders, librarians are constantly receiving pressure from and exerting pressure on their communities to get members to participate, shape, be social, and maximize limited resources. That wouldn't be so bad, except that systems librarians build for their communities are, unlike the communities themselves, far from heterogeneous in nature. Communities are almost always made up of different subcommunities divided by income, location, race, or gender. Businesses and universities are made up of different groups of experts. Online communities are divided by the different levels of participation community members are willing to contribute. Satisfying all of the needs of these different groups or individuals simultaneously, or through one system, is virtually impossible.

For much of the past two centuries, librarians have excused themselves from this reality by claiming some sort of objectivity or lack of bias. The argument is that our systems are equally available to all. But, however widely believed, the notion that librarians build systems that are neutral and don't favor any one part of their communities is simply *not* true.

Remember children's story time at the library? When do librarians offer it? In many public libraries, they offer it in the morning when most parents are at work. Why? According to the Population Reference Bureau, "only 7 percent of all U.S. households consisted of married couples with children in which only one spouse worked. Dual-income families with children made up more than two times as many households."[4] So it would seem these public libraries have decided to offer a service to an elite few families who can afford to have one parent stay at home with their children and bring them to story time—or have their nanny do so. Not exactly a neutral decision.

These competing priorities can be seen in all sorts of places. Take, for example, providing access to scholarly journals in academic libraries, research centers, banks, and so on. Access to these collections is expensive, and getting to be more so. Many librarians realize that helping scholars publish in these journals is an important way to serve their communities. At the same time, they realize that supporting a system where scholars give away their intellectual property rights to publishers, who then turn around and charge these same scholars for access, is problematic, to put it mildly. This system threatens to literally bankrupt colleges and universities. So what do you do, librarian? Do you accept the system as it is while you help scholars publish, or do you try to change the system for the better? Do we show scholars concepts like Open Access publishing, new forms of scholarly engagement (publishing directly to the web, blogging, courseware development), a move to alternative metrics versus increasingly outdated concepts like journal impact factors, the use of institutional repositories, the implementation of library publishing services, and data repositories can not only reduce costs, but can greatly accelerate and enrich scholarly conversation?

As a librarian, you're going to constantly be balancing the divergent and conflicting desires and needs of your community. There will be systems to help you do this, from long-standing practices, to established policies, to power structures within the communities themselves. However, what makes you a librarian—what makes you a professional—is not your ability to set priorities on what is, but to discern what should be.

What Should Be

In chapter 7, we'll delve deeply into the question of balancing different points of view. For now, let me give you two strategies for seeking out guidance from your community in the way you facilitate knowledge creation. The first is to go to the conversation. The second is to focus on the dreams and aspirations of your community members, not their faults.

Go to the Conversation

It was late on a Thursday afternoon when an oncologist told me that I "probably" had cancer—lymphoma to be exact. I remember it distinctly. My wife was in the room and we both went white as ghosts. All I could think about was "I'm going to die."

Without any time to let the news sink in, the doctor also informed us that they had to do a bone marrow biopsy right away because the lab was about to close. Within minutes of being told I most likely had cancer, my wife was whisked out of the room, I was lying face down on my hospital bed, and the oncologist was kneeling on my back and drilling into my pelvis.

After the procedure, my wife returned to the room and we cried, then we pulled out our smartphones and started scouring the Internet for any information we could find on lymphoma.

Let me contrast this to how a diagnosis is delivered in the children's ward one floor above my hospital room. The doctor goes into the child's room with the parents present. He or she then delivers the bad news, much as they had done in my case. However, the doctor has not come alone. The doctor has already talked with a nurse and the children's librarian, bringing them up to speed on the diagnosis and potential treatments. As the doctor reviews the diagnosis, the librarian is writing down the terms used: "lymphoma," "chemo," "marrow," and so on. After the doctor answers the family's initial questions, the librarian goes back to the Family Resources Center (her public work space) and uses her iPad to do Google Searches on the keywords. The iPad has a unique IP number so the search engine doesn't filter the results for a hospital. The children's librarian reviews the top ten hits for each keyword. She then sits down with the parents and goes through each of the results letting them know which sites are ads, which sites are reliable, and why other sites should be avoided. She doesn't stop at Google searches. She brings paired books to the family—picture books for the child (depending on the child's age) and in-depth guides for the parents.

What's my point? I could and did reach out to librarians to help me find information on the latest in research and treatment for my particular kind of cancer. But I'm a professor of library science. What about those patients who aren't? More than that, for the following days and nights, that hospital room was my entire world, jammed with equipment and nurses and two people whose life together was now dramatically different. Everything my wife and I thought and felt about life, death, family, future, career, God—everything was now different—more urgent. No e-mail or tweet could convey my "information needs." What I needed as much as I did journal articles or cancer booklets was recognition of the gravity of that moment.

Every day, people need the help of librarians with issues from child care, to career development, to cancer. And they need our help at the point of need—in their homes, their offices, and their hospital rooms. We can't simply wait for a call; we need to be out in our communities seeking to help. It's only by going to our community members, meeting with them and sitting with them that we can truly see their needs and build systems for them. How can we expect our community members to participate in our systems if we're unwilling to do so in theirs?

Focus on Aspirations, Not Problems

When I tell you to focus on your community members' aspirations rather than their problems, it may sound like something to be sewn onto a conversation pillow, but I assure you it's very practical advice. It's natural for service professionals like librarians to look at the problems of their communities and seek to solve them. After all, if things are going well, do they really need our help? As librarians, we strive to make a difference, to help those who have trouble helping themselves, even in a selfish way, for we need to be needed. Yet focusing on their flaws and deficits will not endear you to your community members. If you truly want them to participate and learn, the strongest motivation you can provide them is to show them how they can become what they aspire to be.

Rather than focus on overcoming illiteracy rates, focus on a creating an educated community. Rather than focus on lawyers who don't know how to do research on expert witnesses, focus on lawyers who can win more cases through better handling of expert witnesses. Rather than focus on cancer, focus on a path to wellness.

The simple truth is aspirational goals are far more motivating and empowering to individuals who must overcome deficits than even the most thoughtful examination of those deficits could ever be. More than that, such goals include a wider segment of a community and thus expand the resources available to help its members actually realize their aspirations.

Take the Free Library of Philadelphia and the homeless community of inner city Philadelphia. Every day, before the library opened, a large crowd of homeless men and woman would congregate in a small park in front of the library. Once the library opened, the homeless would use its bathrooms and gather in its reading rooms for warmth. The homeless population got so large that they began disrupting other community members and services at the library. The librarians reached out to other public libraries for help and suggestions.

There was a great deal of advice on setting stricter policies, vagrancy laws, and working with law enforcement to keep the homeless population out of—and away from—the library. There were architectural and design suggestions: get rid of outside benches, put spikes on surfaces that people could sit on, install a sprinkler system to deter loitering on the front lawn. In essence, there was a lot of advice on how to deal with the "homeless problem."

The librarians of the Free Library chose to take a different tack. Rather than focus on the homeless as a problem, they chose instead to look at the benefits to the community if it mobilized and tended to its greatest asset: its citizens. Social services began to go to the small park in front of the library to offer the homeless meals, coats, and health care. The librarians hired homeless men and woman to be bathroom attendants—keeping the facilities clean and providing paying jobs. Then they opened a café.

The café was funded by the Bank of America, headquartered in the city. The coffee and equipment were provided by Starbucks. Local bakeries provided the pastries for the café, meaning the library wasn't competing with local businesses but helping them. And the café was staffed by men and women in a homelessness-to-work program.

Instead of dwelling on the "homeless problem," the librarians created a positive opportunity to increase service to their community members with a café, generate positive publicity for corporations, increase revenue for local businesses, and give homeless men and woman a chance to get off the street. And though the librarians didn't eliminate homelessness in Philadelphia, they helped to alleviate it, and, more important, they helped their community do good and do well at the same time.

Librarianship is a noble profession, not because of its long and sometimes distinguished history, but because, every day, we librarians choose to make things better, even if it's one café at a time. Librarians improve society, some days by inches, some days by miles, but always in a principled way. Which brings us to perhaps the most complex issue we will tackle: just what exactly does "improve society" mean?

7 Improve Society

Core Chapter Concept: Librarians shape and then enact their communities' definitions of improvement.

Here are two myths that exist simultaneously in librarianship:

1. Librarians are unbiased and provide equitable access to all in their systems (services, programs, collections);
2. Communities should dictate the systems of librarians.

The first myth we've addressed head-on. In seeking to increase the knowledge of your community members, your approach, the language you use, the way you organize things, even your gender and race all play a role in how you design systems and in how and to whom you provide services. The second myth, however, is equally untrue. Whether you call it "user-based design" or "community-led librarianship," allowing your community to dictate your systems still comes down to abdicating your professional responsibility to improve society.

As we've just seen, the way you design systems needs community participation, but you facilitate that participation. You choose which community voices to listen to, which aspirations merit your attention. Since knowledge creation is a conversation, you also have a voice in that conversation.

Let me give a seemingly trivial example. In a workshop about meeting community needs, one librarian stated flatly that she refused to print out Wikipedia articles for school-age kids. This led to a bit of an uproar, with the familiar protestations of the need for librarians to be unbiased in providing information to their community members. The librarian went on to say that she didn't print them out because "the teachers decided that students would lose points if they cited Wikipedia. If I helped students do this, I would, in essence, be helping students lower their grades."

In another setting, a library director decided to filter Internet access on the library's public access terminals because the police, in attempting to catch sex offenders violating their parole, had taken to standing and watching community members use the terminals. This was having a chilling effect far worse than any filter might. The library's filter allowed the police to leave because now the offending activity couldn't take place on the library's terminals (at least not as far as the police knew, but just ask any fifteen-year-old how easy it is to bypass an Internet filter), and community members could again use the terminals without someone looking over their shoulder.

Neither of these librarians was being unbiased, and both chose to support one view of improvement in their communities over others. But there's that word again, "chose." As professionals, we make choices, and, in doing so, we shape the communities we serve. Just as there is pressure for participation exerted by community members on the librarian, there is needed an equal pressure exerted by librarians on the community. This pressure comes from the third defining aspect of librarianship: the librarian's values,

A librarian is defined by a mission, a set of facilitating tools, and a set of values that underlie the entire profession. These values are:

- service;
- learning;
- openness;
- intellectual freedom and safety; and
- intellectual honesty.

Forged over millennia, these values are still being debated and reframed. Yet, even though they may vary in their wording and emphasis, the values have served our profession well, and allowed it to serve communities whether in colleges or on street corners in the world of white male privilege or that of protesting black citizens in Baltimore. They are at the core of how librarians responded to civil unrest in Alexandria, Egypt, and in Ferguson, Missouri. The values of librarians are not those of liberals or conservatives, Democrats or Republicans; they are the values of knowledge professionals seeking to improve our communities. And they represent the collective, agreed-upon biases of our profession.

Service

If there is one common theme in how librarians seek to serve our communities and society as a whole, it is empowerment. Librarians promote many kinds of literacy—reading, mathematical, information, media—as a means of empowering our community members to have greater control in their lives. What all these kinds of literacy have in common is an ability to detect patterns in some dynamic environments and to make best use of those patterns. Thus, in enhancing or building our community members' literacy, librarians are empowering them—giving them greater power to control their situations.

Here's the thing, the only way you can empower someone is to first empower yourself. You can't teach someone to read unless you read. You can't help someone find and use resources unless you have some proficiency in information seeking. To empower, we librarians must become powerful. Not powerful to impose our views on others, but powerful to make others powerful. In this model, librarians serve as stewards for our communities. We steward our communities' resources and allocated power (through a charter or a budget line) to achieve some mutually agreed-upon end. We are "of the community" in that both we and our communities have a voice in how that stewardship is accomplished, and, most important, both benefit from the stewardship. As librarians, we have a stake in our communities improving because when they improve so does our own standing and thus also our ability to be of greater service.

There is, however, another, older model of service promoted in librarianship: the servant model, according to which librarians are community servants, who should have limited autonomy, little voice, and little power. Such a view is not without some justification. Indeed, there is ample historical precedent to be skeptical of librarians imposing their views on those they are meant to serve.

Thus, when public libraries emerged in the United States, they very much supported a dominant, restrictive view of learning, the view primarily of well-to-do white males, who believed that fiction played no part in learning, and who sought to limit access to resources to only the "right" resources. Many in Europe are still fearful of librarians having too much power, harking back to the rise of fascism when libraries as government instruments sought to perpetuate a single point of view. To be clear, even now, there are many who feel libraries and universities are part of the suppression of "dangerous" ideas by the rich and powerful.

In the servant model, librarians are also facilitators, but in a passive, unbiased way; they don't empower people—rather, people empower themselves. And if people have no power, can't read, can't access the Internet, can't vote, can't determine their own destinies, so the philosophy behind this model goes, it was their choice not to have power.

I have to agree that, just because librarians seek to empower individuals or communities doesn't mean those individuals or communities have to accept that power. Ultimately, taking power, like learning, is a matter of choice. But where I fundamentally disagree with this philosophy is its assumption that all individuals are presented with the same choices. There is obviously a larger issue of social equity or "social justice" (to use a more loaded term) at play here. If you live in Detroit, a city in bankruptcy today, you don't have the same choices as someone who lives in Ann Arbor, a relatively affluent university town nearby. You'll have access to fewer libraries; your urban schools will underperform. Can you overcome these obstacles on your own? Some people can. The media are replete with stories of people who have, most often with the help of mentors or heroes who made it all possible—but such people are the exceptions to the rule.

For generations, a plethora of factors have effectively robbed people of their choices: poverty and discrimination based on race, ethnicity, religion, gender, or sexual orientation, to name the most significant factors. To say that people have always had the same choices to empower themselves is to ignore the massive changes in opportunities brought about by the civil rights movement, women's liberation, and child labor laws, to mention only a few of the most important social developments in the last century or so. If we, as a society, truly believe that all people are created equal, and that all people deserve an equal chance at success, then we are honor bound to do what we can to establish a level playing field of empowerment. And if you believe, as I do, that librarians support equitable access to knowledge and the democratic process, we must first seek the power to make that support count.

The world we live in is too complex to simply say people choose to be illiterate, or poor, or powerless. Certainly, some few do. But many more do not. And those who choose to read need teachers willing to share their power of reading. Those who choose to fight their way out of poverty need those willing to provide them with online access to job opportunities when, even to be a janitor, you must submit an online application. And those guaranteed the right to vote need those willing to show them how to obtain voter documentation and how to register regardless of their political affiliation. Without this empowering assistance, they have no real choices. Only the illusion of choice.

And so we come full circle to librarians and service. Do librarians seek power? Yes, we do, but in order to empower the individuals and communities and institutions we serve. And only in accordance with a set of professional values. Is the power we acquire neutral? No power is neutral—all power comes from some inequality. You are powerful on the playing field because you're faster or stronger than other players. Your business is powerful because it makes bigger profits or better products than other businesses. And you are powerful as a librarian because your skills and expertise are greater than those of the members you seek to empower and you are seen as highly credible. You are not a neutral resource to your community—you are a trusted resource.

Learning

Lifelong learning is a core value of librarians. This is reflected not only in the services we provide, but also in how we conduct ourselves as librarians. We are constantly learning both about the subjects of interest to the communities we serve and also about librarianship itself. As a librarian, you must be part of the ongoing discourse of the values and systems librarians build. How can you expect your community to be efficient and effective learners (knowledge creators) if you yourself don't model that behavior?

Note that that the entire chapter on knowledge creation (chapter 4) and maintaining a pragmatic approach to knowledge applies to you as much as it does to your community members. Dogma and untested assumptions have no place in our profession. We honor the librarians who came before us not by memorializing their systems and behaviors, but by constantly questioning and often improving upon them.

Openness

Librarians believe the best decisions come from the richest pool of inputs (voices, resources, media, etc.). This translates into many practices and beliefs, which is why diversity is so important to librarians (but sadly so rarely achieved). Inputs on systems, decisions, and conversations should represent a cross-section of your community members. Differences in race, gender, social status, and educational background should be welcome and celebrated in the work of librarians.

Openness is also about transparency. The work of librarians should be open to community comment and, of course, participation. Take the example of Justin Hoenke. When, as coordinator of Teen Services at the Chattanooga Public Library, Justin got a 3-D printer for his programs, rather than retreat to his office to figure out how to put it together and make it work, he moved the printer to a desk right in the middle of teen area. As people would pass by, he would invite them to help build and operate the printer. He wanted to figure out how the printer worked, of course, but, more than that, he wanted the process of learning to be open and to serve as an example to staff and community members (especially younger members) alike.

This quest for transparency and openness can be seen in the push of librarians to make scholarly publishing more open and available to all scholars—both inside and outside the academy. Librarians keep archives of information about government and business activities for greater accountability of both public and private officials. Although not every context allows for complete public dissemination of information about businesses and the government (not proprietary knowledge or classified work, for example), librarians always push for the maximum distribution and access to such information.

Intellectual Freedom and Safety

My frequent use of "professional" in this guide is meant to constantly remind you that a librarian is not some clerk mindlessly applying predetermined tools and procedures. To be a professional is to make decisions, work through ambiguity, and balance competing priorities. This can even be seen in our core values. Although librarians seek transparency and the maximum disclosure of information and ideas, experience has shown that there is one area where wide disclosure can be neither appropriate nor desirable: the privacy of our community members.

As librarians, we believe that the systems we create (like libraries) must be safe places to explore dangerous ideas. If indeed the best decisions come from the richest pool of inputs, then there will be a time when one community member needs to engage with people and resources that might be frowned on by other community members. We protect our members' rights to engage with these ideas. It is only in a place (whether physical or virtual) where they feel truly safe that they can learn without inhibition.

Here, however, I have to once again invoke our professionalism. Many in our profession see privacy in binary terms, as a sort of absolute. But privacy is more nuanced. Many studies show how people, particularly the young, have come to see privacy as a sort of commodity. They trade their privacy, or at least part of their privacy, for service. For example, they are willing to have a company like Amazon remember what items they have purchased over time to avoid rebuying the same items. Users of Facebook have long ago realized that price of Facebook's capabilities comes at the cost of their posts and likes being sold to advertisers.

As a professional, you must work hand in glove with your community members on where their privacy can be compromised for service, while doing your best to preserve their privacy from further disclosure. Today, all too often, librarians claim member privacy as sacrosanct even as they deploy third-party systems (discovery tools, article databases, and such) that regularly track member activity. In doing so, librarians foster a false perception of privacy that neither serves their members well nor bodes well for the credibility enjoyed by librarians.

Intellectual Honesty

Although you have your own views and biases, you should acknowledge and disclose them wherever possible. As a reflective professional, you must constantly seek out alternative views and try to understand how your viewpoint might affect the services you provide to others.

Note, however, this doesn't mean that you have to see all views as equally valid. Having been trained in library science, you take the scientific approach to knowledge and belief. Some call this a "rational approach." It comes down to understanding that there are rational, scientific methods we can use to try to uncover the truth of things.

Note the qualifying "try to" in "try to uncover the truth of things." Scientists and librarians are on a never-ending quest for the truth. As we saw in chapter 4, the scientific method that has been so powerful in pushing forward human achievement is designed to develop not the only, not the true, but the most likely explanation of a phenomenon, until such time as a better (more scientific) explanation comes along.

That said, realize that true science emerges not from a linear rational approach to a problem, but from a thick froth of argument, hunches, passions, and obsessions. Also, realize that, as much as we try, there are some topics that simply don't lend themselves to a scientific approach. This means that, as librarians, we should not dismiss new ideas out of hand, however far-fetched, "unscientific," or unsafe they might seem, and that we must always provide a safe place to explore and discuss unsafe ideas.

We've now explored the three major factors that define a librarian:

1. Our mission: to improve society through facilitating knowledge creation in our communities;

2. Our means of achieving that mission: facilitating two-way access to conversations and resources to spark conversations; building knowledge; providing a safe environment; and building on the motivations of our community members; and

3. The core values that underlie our work: service, learning, openness, intellectual freedom and safety, and intellectual honesty.

In chapter 8, we'll put this all together to flesh out just what a librarian is.

8 Librarians

Core Chapter Concept: Librarians are principled professionals working with their communities in transformative social engagement.

We can now answer the question we started with in chapter 2, "What is a librarian?" A librarian is on a mission to improve society. To accomplish this mission, librarians use a set of tools to facilitate knowledge creation; they build participatory systems; and they empower their community members in accordance with the core values of service, learning, openness, intellectual freedom and safety, and intellectual honesty. These aspects of librarianship reveal the kinship of today's librarians with those building libraries as far back as the Babylonians.

Our world, of course, is quite different from the Babylonians'. Not simply because of the Internet and our new technological tools. Advances in public health (a safe food and water supply, indoor plumbing, vaccinations) in the nineteenth and twentieth centuries and the increase in life expectancy from 54 to 75 over the past fifty years,[1] for example, have had a much greater effect on librarianship than Facebook or Twitter ever could.. No, this is about a constant renegotiation of what it means to be a librarian and serve the communities of today. As we've seen, professions like farming, teaching, and librarianship have stood the test of time because they have constantly applied long-standing values and missions to ever-changing tools and opportunities.

Before we get into the specifics of what a librarian should know, we need to address the issue of entrance requirements. How do you become a librarian? There are three means of entering our profession: by degree, by hire, and by spirit.

The first and predominant means of becoming a professional librarian is to get a degree in librarianship. In North America, and in many parts of Europe, this means getting a master's degree in library science (or library and information science). In the United States, these graduate programs are accredited by the American Library Association; accredited degrees are required by many libraries and often required by law.

The second means of becoming a librarian—by hire—is simply to be hired with the title "librarian." The past few Librarians of Congress, for example, had no degree in librarianship. There are plenty of small public libraries run by people with no graduate degree. In parts of rural New England, for example, where a library director could never earn enough to pay off the debt incurred in getting a master's degree in library science, the director is not required to have one. Librarians by hire often bring skills from other disciplines and do a lot of on-the-job learning supported by state libraries and library associations.

Those who become librarians by the third means—by spirit—don't have a library degree and may not even have the word "librarian" in their job title, but they clearly have the same mission, skill set, and service outlook as professional librarians. People like Brewster Kahle, an early Internet entrepreneur and a librarian by spirit who has devoted his energy and a good part of his accrued wealth to building a free digital library of everything on the web as part of his efforts to facilitate knowledge creation in communities.[2]

There is a tension in our profession between people who become librarians by these three different means. Librarians by degree often feel their education better prepares them for our profession and lack respect for librarians by hire or by spirit. For their part, some librarians by hire and by spirit feel that a degree doesn't adequately prepare a person for the realities of librarianship in the field. Some librarians by spirit hate the title "librarian," feeling it restricts their job opportunities. I could spend quite some time on the differences between these three avenues to our profession (and have done so in *The Atlas of New Librarianship* and *Expect More*), but, ultimately, it doesn't matter how you become a librarian so long as you have the mission, the means, and the values of our profession.

With that out of the way, let's get down to business. What do you need to know to do your job as a librarian?

The Salzburg Curriculum

To answer that question, a group of librarians and museum professionals from around the world gathered in Salzburg, Austria, in October 2011. The Salzburg Global Seminar and the U.S. Institute of Museum and Library Services cohosted a gathering, "Libraries and Museums in an Era of Participatory Culture."[3]

Representatives from North and South America, Asia, the Middle East, Europe, Africa, and Australia came together to talk about how more and more libraries and museums were looking beyond their collections and artifacts to their communities. They shared stories about collected tribal masks still used in ceremonies, the Arab Spring, and seismic shifts in research libraries.

One subgroup met to talk about the skills needed by librarians and museum professionals to do their jobs. They came up with the "Salzburg Curriculum," which was later expanded and revised into the form presented here. The curriculum is not intended to be a course list for a master's program, but rather a set of guiding competencies that can shape both graduate programs for and the ongoing professional development of librarians and museum professionals alike.

It begins with a framing statement:

The mission of librarians and museum professionals is to foster conversations that improve society through knowledge exchange and social action. One of the unique aspects of this curricular framework is that it sees the preparation of librarians and museum professionals in a unified way. Despite ongoing discussions of the links between the two professions, these connections are rarely, if ever, seen in how each group is prepared for their work.

This framework is dedicated to lifelong learning both in and out of formal educational settings. It is intended to be applied to continuing education as well—not just degree programs.

The curricular topics are driven by the following core values (in no particular order):

- Openness and transparency
- Self-reflection
- Collaboration
- Service
- Empathy and respect
- Continuous learning/striving for excellent (which requires lifelong learning)
- Creativity and imagination

If the curriculum's language on mission and values seems similar to the language in this guide, it's no coincidence—I was a member of the subgroup that drafted it. In any case, the framing statement sets out global concerns and directions. The curriculum then goes on to specify a set of key areas of knowledge ("curricular topics"):

• Transformative Social Engagement
• Technology
• Management for Participation (Professional Competencies)
• Asset Management
• Cultural Skills
• Knowledge, Learning, and Innovation[4]

In the following sections and tables, I'll provide the specific skills outlined by the Salzburg Curriculum with my own emphasis and often my own wording as well. I'll then expand on some ideas and ways of interpreting these skills in the context of our understandings of librarianship to this point.

Transformative Social Engagement

Skills	Discussion
Activism and advocacy	Librarians need to identify key issues within their communities that call for wider support. They need to directly advocate for these issues and to prepare community members to be their own advocates.
Social responsibility	Librarians have a social responsibility to their communities; in actively facilitating knowledge creation, they must recognize how they affect those communities, sometimes unintentionally.
Critical social analysis	Librarians need to critically analyze what is happening within their communities. They must go beyond simple demographics and surveys to true understanding.
System creation in context	Librarians need to determine how a system fits into a larger community's needs and aspirations.
Sustainability of societal mission	Librarians need to determine how resources are going to be allocated to systems and what kind of promotions will be in place to ensure the success of those systems.
Conflict management	Librarians need to facilitate and moderate conversations that arise from conflict and, if possible, to help others reach common ground.

As a librarian, you need to understand that you have a *social responsibility*; your actions and your position within your community—your *trusted* position within your community—are great responsibilities. You must understand that librarians are role models in the world of knowledge creation: you affect how your community members think and learn. You must also prepare them to be socially responsible.

For many in our profession, this curricular topic and its associated skills represent the biggest departure from "traditional" or institutional librarianship. For too long have librarians talked about improving their communities and empowering their members while describing themselves as "unbiased" or "objective." Service requires you to make decisions, to prioritize one activity over another, for example, or to select one resource over another. No longer can librarians believe they do good in society without recognizing that they actively shape both what that good and what society are.

Technology

Skills	Discussion
Reachng Out	Librarians must reach out to, and learn *with*, their communities.
Engaging and evolving with technologies	Librarians must constantly evaluate new technologies to determine which are most useful to their communities.
Imparting technology skills to communities across generations	Librarians must find ways to reach across the divides of access, age, knowledge, environment, and motivation in their communities.
Creating and maintaining an effective virtual presence	Librarians must keep up with technologies in order to maintain an effective virtual presence within their communities regardless of space and time.

All of these technical skills come down to acknowledging that, as a librarian, you must support conversations within your community not only in person, but also online (and, increasingly, in hybrid environments that mix the physical and the virtual). This means the systems you build, the programs you offer, the products you create, the support you provide must utilize the tools of modern technology wherever appropriate.

Does this mean every librarian should be able to code? No, it doesn't, but some should. Does every librarian need to learn every new tech tool? No, but you should be willing to play with new technologies (more on that in a moment). It means that librarianship, at its heart, is a technical profession. From card catalogs to virtual reality, you must always be on the lookout for new tools to fulfill our mission. You also need to be able to match the changing needs of your community with changing tools.

The real trick is in how you develop and maintain your technical skills both to advance your own knowledge and to better support the community members you serve, even as, in doing so, you learn to better understand their needs and aspirations. Remember the story told in chapter 7 of Justin Hoenke, who built and learned about a 3-D printer in the middle of the teen area of the Chattanooga Public Library? He was clearly engaging with new technologies and learning. However, by doing this in public with his community members, he was also helping them learn. As part of that process and the discussions that arose, Justin could better understand the current tech level of his members and could generate ideas on how technology of that level could be put to best use. Service and learning bound together.

One librarian referred to this as moving from serving a community member "across the desk" to serving "by sitting beside the member." The librarian also said it was the scariest professional thing she'd ever done. In her case, she was experimenting with robotics kits and how to use them in children's programs. Normally, she would have retreated to her office (or home), figured out the technology, and only then, when she was fully confident in her ability would she have brought in her community members. This might have made her feel safe, but it would have robbed her members of a chance for authentic learning. Instead, she chose to model that *everyone*—librarian and community members alike—should learn together, at the same time, and she even demonstrated that false starts and frustration are part of the learning process.

The other great part of learning technology side by side with community members is that it prevents undue attachment to any given tool. Let's face it, the geeks among us (I count myself as one of them) tend to romanticize new tools and technologies. A new iPhone seems to hold an infinite amount of opportunity. However, to some, it represents the unwitting adoption of a closed technology system with Apple as faceless corporate controller of their private information. By learning and evaluating technology in public, you recruit a band of geeks, but you also expose yourself to healthy skeptics. Teach by learning, try by collaborating. Your credibility and respect in the community come from your transparency and openness, not by your ability to "know it all."

Asset Management

Skills	Discussion
Preserve/safeguard	Preservation is seen as the protection of an item removed from its regular use. Safeguarding acknowledges that, in many settings, artifacts are still very much in use (from ceremonial garb to fishing poles), and they must be maintained for continued use.
Collect	A collection should reflect a constant dialogue with the community. What is important and unimportant? To whom is it important? When is it important? How can librarians build and share ideas?

Although librarianship is about facilitation and knowledge creation, it often involves collecting things (books, software, documents, robots, ideas, experts) to get the job done. This means librarians should know how to collect, organize, and safeguard those things.

In most libraries, you might collect books; in other settings, software licenses. Some librarians build and manage living collections, like the librarians in Wisconsin public libraries who manage collections of fishing poles, which must not only be bar coded, but also cleaned and strung to make sure they're ready for use. Does this mean that if you were to manage such a collection, you'd need to be a fishing expert? No, you might instead recruit a community expert to do the actual maintenance. Remember, the community you serve is your real collection.

That local communities should have a say in the form and structure of asset management for their libraries is true even in the most traditional of settings. Many librarians are migrating from the librarian-oriented Dewey Decimal Classification system to locally developed schema. Rather than looking for 100s and 200s, community members can now shift through topics like "thrillers," and "steampunk."

The organizational skills of librarians (metadata creation, indexing, classification) are ways of thinking about collections, *not* rote application of tools like the Dewey Decimal System or Machine Readable Cataloging (MARC). There is no universal way to organize things. Librarians focus on organizing them in ways that make sense to their local communities, but that can be shared globally. If trying to accomplish local and global usage at one and the same time seems like a contradiction to you, it's because you're still thinking in analog terms, where one datum has to rest in one place. In the digital world, application programming interfaces (APIs) and modern metadata systems (XML, RDF) can link data from one locality to another. Does this mean you should include mastery of metadata systems among your core librarian skills? Yes, it does.

Cultural Skills

Skills	Discussion
Communication	You must understand how and when to communicate, and that different communities will associate different terms and meanings to things.
Intercultural	"Intercultural" was chosen over "multicultural" to focus on interaction between diverse communities. How can you help bring these diverse groups together?
Languages/terminology	To truly interact with your community, you must be aware of the different languages and terminologies associated with its various ethnic and other groups.
Support for multiple types of literacies	You must also be aware of different learning styles and the fact that most people benefit from a mixture of different learning approaches.

Librarians are in the knowledge creation business. Knowledge is created through conversation. Therefore librarians are in the conversation business. At the core of the work we do is communication. So why not just call these skills "communication skills"? Because the terms we use are as much cultural markers as they are means of transmitting meaning.

Take, for example, the terms "catalogs" and "databases." Most people interpret them as "things at the library that aren't as easy to use as Google." Why do these terms persist? Because they have become part of the library culture. You'll recall our discussion of L_1 and L_0 language from chapter 4. Although we use "L_1"and "L_0" to allow us to communicate faster and more effectively, terms like these can also exclude people from conversations.

Communication and language are deeply intertwined with the culture that uses them. Take as an example the events in Ferguson, Missouri, we talked about at the start of chapter 1. What do you call them: "riots" or "protests"? Some people see the two terms as practically interchangeable, but, to many, especially to those in Ferguson, the term "riots" represents violence of any kind, whether justified or not, whereas the term "protests" acknowledges some underlying wrong.

As librarians, we have to make sure that we choose and apply terms that have some currency in our communities. And we must understand how terms are used in the communities we seek to serve. That is why even though I use "member" for those we serve as librarians, what you call your community members should be whatever you and the community agree. Allies, neighbors, faculty, clients, makers—that is part of building a service that respects local culture.

Language is just one way librarians understand culture. Deborah Turner, a professor at Drexel University looks at another: the modes we use to communicate. She studies oral cultures. For example, many underserved populations in our cities strongly rely upon an oral tradition when seeking out knowledge. The first thing someone in these populations does is to look for the right person to ask. As a former president of the Italian library association once put it: "In America, when you want to make sauce, you read a cookbook. In Italy, we ask our mothers." Unless the systems you build take these cultural factors into account, you won't be able to adequately serve your community; indeed, you may even alienate your community members. As a librarian, you must learn to listen and spend time learning alongside your members before you jump in to make your systems.

Many attending community colleges are first-time college students who come there later in life after not fitting into the traditional school regime. They often need special help to bring their basic and study skills up to speed for the classroom. One community college built a large and successful face-to-face tutoring service for just that reason. When, however, with the advent of the Iraq and Afghanistan wars, the college attempted to better serve its now remote military students by moving its tutoring service online, its success rate fell precipitously. Why? It turns out that, even though the content of the tutoring was the same, its mode of delivery was very different: sitting face-to-face with a tutor was replaced with online readings and text-based exercises. Nontraditional students, who preferred interpersonal oral conversations, suddenly had to cope with written ones, with much poorer results.

Knowledge, Learning, and Innovation

Skills	Discussion
Construction of knowledge	Librarians must start knowledge creation where a community member is, not assume every community member recognizes a universal truth.
Innovation	Librarians must constantly look for ways to improve the systems that serve their communities, adapting ideas from across industries and communities.
Interpretation	Because an object or a piece of information means different things to different people, librarians must find ways to interpret these things to people with different viewpoints.
Dissemination	Librarians must not only bring the world's ideas to their communities; they must also actively seek to bring the ideas of their communities to the larger world.
Promotion of information literacy	Librarians must help community members identify relevant sources of knowledge, extract concepts from them, integrate these concepts into larger concepts, and evaluate the effectiveness of this process.

Because much of this guide is devoted to knowledge and learning, I'm going to focus on innovation here. Why, you may ask, is innovation grouped in with learning and knowledge anyway? The short answer is that innovation is positive change and a unique application of what you know to a given problem, process, or system. Both learning and innovation then are about improvement. Importantly, both learning and innovation come in very different scales.

I reminded students of this in an introduction to the field course for new librarians. As part of the course, I set up an anonymous discussion board where students could post questions and comments they didn't feel comfortable raising in class surrounded by their peers. One student posted,

"While I think I could be a great librarian, I don't consider myself to be innovative. I'm great when someone gives me a task. Can't I just be a good worker bee?" My answer is no. Innovation is central to our profession. How can we expect our communities to be constantly learning and engaged in improving society if we as librarians can't innovate to help them do so?

Now, that said, we don't all have to be like Steve Jobs or Thomas Edison to be innovators. As with words like "protests," "catalogs," and indeed "librarian," the word "innovation" is defined by society. Innovation is very much about making things better, big and small. Not only that, but, unlike inventions, many innovations are new applications of known—old—items to meet new situations. Librarians are innovators in that they are always looking to make processes more effective.

I had one librarian who married her two loves together and created "yoga story time" complete with "downward dog" and "scary monster" poses. Betsy Kennedy and her librarian colleagues started story time in a local food pantry in Cazenovia, New York. While working with the kids, they became aware that the children weren't the only ones in need of literacy activities, and so they started to hold high school equivalency classes for the parents. When it also became clear that this need existed all over the county, they teamed up with churches to extend the program across the region. All of these initiatives are innovative because they are ways that librarians pay attention to their communities' needs and incorporate good ideas to better serve them.

I should also note that Betsy's service, while it could be seen as solving problems in her community, it was really about helping citizens achieve their aspirations. The librarians didn't fix a literacy problem, they empowered better parents. The librarians of Madison County didn't fix children who couldn't read, they created children of worth. During the service Betsy was giving out new books to the children in the program. One of the girls started to cry. When Betsy asked what was the matter, the girl said, "This is the first new thing I have ever owned." That book wasn't about reading, that book was a tool for a child creating the knowledge that she mattered.

This last story highlights how, to innovate, we must sometimes break out of our cultural confines. Viewed through fresh eyes, story time can be as innovative as assembling and operating 3-D printers and massive metadata repositories, or even more so. Indeed, too many librarians, educators, and city officials seek to be innovative by adopting the Silicon Valley culture of the startup. But, in doing so, these people are being far from innovative—instead of leading, they are following. What's more, creating apps that require high-speed Internet access and up-to-date computers and development environments is hardly the way out of poverty for those who can barely afford phones much less food.

What's needed is a unique culture of innovation, grounded both in a creative ethos and in the culture of your community, one that highlights your community's abilities and that celebrates its contributions. The Silicon Valley culture represents a type of people and set of goals unique to a particular time and place. It is a culture where technological creativity and economic gain are the foremost goals. Can we learn from this culture? Certainly, but it's hardly the only culture that innovates. And its goals are hardly the goals of every community.

Here in upstate New York, an apple farm named "Beak & Skiff" has over the years transformed itself from a pick-your-own apple orchard on the side of the road to a truly unique eco-tourism destination. You can still pick apples, but now you can also taste different apple ciders (hard and soft) and apple vodkas. You can buy apple pies and other local apple delicacies. You can taste dozens of apple varieties, all while having a gourmet lunch and listening to live music in the middle of farmland. Beak & Skiff took what it knew well, growing apples, and used it to innovate—to grow itself into what it is today. And it did so without having to build its own apple app.

As librarians, we should all be innovators, and we should seek out innovators in our communities. If our innovations are to have long-lasting effects, they must take into account the culture of our communities. An innovation doesn't have to be huge: it can shave minutes off a process or it can save pennies in a transaction, but, big or small, innovations move communities forward. There is, however, one important thing you must keep in mind—the outcomes of any innovation are unpredictable. Those few seconds saved, those few pennies saved add up; they can make your community freer to risk and experiment, which, in turn, can lead to massive shifts. We'll return to this when we talk about how the libraries that librarians build can support innovation and entrepreneurship.

Management for Participation

Skills	Discussion
Furthering institutional sustainability	How can you help align librarian-built systems to your larger organization's vision and goals, whether as an employee or as a project partner?
Institutional advocacy	Having advocated within the community you serve, how can you advocate for yourself, your profession, and your institution or organization?
Economic management	How can you help manage finances and budgeting in your institution or organization?
Applying ethics and values	How can you apply the basic values of librarianship to everyday situations?
Sharing	How can you effectively circulate and improve upon ideas within your organization or community.
Collaboration	How can you effectively work with peers and in interdisciplinary teams? How can you form partnerships with community members and other experts?
Assessment	Which systems are successful, and which systems should be retired? Assessment, analysis, and consideration of overall impact are necessary managerial skills for a librarian.

Most of the skills listed in the table above are self-explanatory, but the topic of advocacy merits further attention. What follows is a discussion by Wendy Newman, who has been both an outspoken advocate for librarians and a teacher of the advocacy process itself. Wendy has looked very deeply into the idea of librarians and advocacy, even teaching a massive open online course (MOOC) on the topic in 2015.

Advocacy and Librarianship
by Wendy Newman

Librarianship as defined in this guide is rich in advocacy strength and potential. Why? Because librarianship is steeped in community, and because advocacy is all about relationships. Great librarianship and great advocacy are not about the survival of libraries as institutions, or indeed about any institutions, but about the improvement of society. As we know, the specific community in which we are facilitating knowledge creation can be a city or town, a neighborhood, a college or university, a school, a law or business firm, a government department. What great librarians have in common in all these settings is an outward-looking focus, a body of knowledge and ethics, and an activist approach. This outward and activist orientation is essential to our role as advocates.

Quite simply, we need the support of others. This support may be policy (e.g., policy that affirms and protects privacy and intellectual freedom). It often is financial support (for salaries, data, or physical facilities). Or it may be for partnership commitments within or outside a community. Though we've had a historical tendency in this profession to believe that our work is self-evidently worthy of support, the cold reality is that, without an intentional focus on advocacy, we may be invisible to those whose support we need. And decisions are made in a highly contentious environment, one in which many good things compete for support. We can't afford to demonize or dismiss decision makers as ignorant cost cutters. And we shouldn't dismiss advocacy as too "political," too commercial, or too specialized for us. In the past, our communities have suffered from timidity, reluctance, or uncertainty in our advocacy. Perhaps we just didn't see it as our job.

We do now. The Salzburg Curriculum, in setting forth the competencies needed by future library and museum professionals in an ever more participatory environment, is clear about this: advocacy is a component of transformative social engagement. In this view, competence in advocacy entails both advocating for the community and helping others to become advocates.

Enter librarians as advocates because it's not enough for us to carry out the work of librarianship without continuously and intentionally engaging the support that's necessary. We're not talking here of promotion for increased use of our services, though it's not a bad idea to make a bigger difference in volume of service. We're talking, instead, about support for increasing our capacity.

Having agreed that advocacy is essential, how do we do it? Research and experience both affirm some basics.

• First things first: people do things for their reasons, not our reasons. Like librarianship, advocacy is all about what's important to *them*. We need to understand their reasons.

• It may seem blindingly obvious, but we need to know who has the power to make the decision we seek, and who and what influences them. Usually, the most important decision makers are few in number. So we waste time if we try to convince "everyone."

• To understand and respond to what is important to those who make policy, financial, or partnership decisions, we must get into conversation with them, and listen to what they have to say. Then we reflect back to them the ways in which we match their priorities.

• The people who use a service and those who will go to bat for it are different people. This may be surprising, but it's true. We have research on this. When seeking support, therefore, engage as advocates those most likely to step up.[5] Generally, these are activists who have a long history of involvement and who are connected with many others (Malcolm Gladwell calls them "Connectors" and "Mavens").[6]

• We have to position our cause in terms of what's important to our audience, not to us. If they care about improving early childhood reading readiness, for example, we need to position our work in that area as an asset worthy of engagement and support, and use their language when we talk with them about it.

• We must frame the case in the community's interests, using the community's situation and aspirations as our starting point. How do we know about the community members' aspirations? We've talked with them, we've heard them, and we're able to use their language.

• It's all about relationships. Advocates build relationships of credibility and trust with decision makers and those who influence them. After all, we're more inclined to believe those with whom we already have trusting relationships. Credibility is earned incrementally, and it's never automatic.

• Passion matters. Librarians who are passionate and engaged in their communities are, according to research, most likely to engage the support of others.

• Advocates must have both data and stories, and know how to insert them opportunely. Stories of transformative impact are memorable; they give life to data. But data are fundamental to accountability, and they are more effective with some decision makers than stories. As data librarian extraordinaire Kimberly Silk says, "You need data and stories. The data make the stories real and the stories make the data matter."

• In an environment of "noise," people cope by simplifying. Therefore, advocates must convey their messages in short, personal, memorable, and powerful sound bites..

Thus librarians' advocacy draws on the same foundations as New Librarianship: relationship development, activist views, consultation and conversation, respect for others' views and priorities, and a focus on aspirations. For the librarian who is focused on the long game, it's an ethical responsibility as well.

Assessment

How do you approach assessment in librarianship? It all depends. That may seem odd to librarians who've been in the field for any length of time. After all, there's been a tremendous amount of good research into how we evaluate collections and reference services. We have developed a huge number of measures (circulation numbers, gate counts), deep discussions of assessment approaches (outcome-based measures, impact factors), and even large-scale assessment projects (LibQual). But how do you assess the "completeness" of collections that are idiosyncratic to particular communities, like the New York City library's collection of building materials or the Wisconsin public libraries' collections of fishing poles? How do you assess the Ann Arbor library's collection of everything from synthesizers and musical instruments to looms and spinning wheels?

What's more almost all of these metrics means, and projects apply to institutional libraries, not the work of librarians across the full range of contexts and work settings. Does gate count make sense to an embedded librarian? Why do I care about collection coverage if I didn't build one to serve my community?

There are ways you can learn how to assess the work of librarians outside of the context in which they work. First, you need to focus on methods of assessment over using specific metrics. And you need to master both quantitative and qualitative methods of assessment. You need to learn how to do surveys (and that there are many settings where surveys make no sense) and how to form focus groups. And, increasingly, you also need to learn how to explore and visualize data sets. These kinds of skills will give you the flexibility you need to assess what whatever system you may build with your community.

There are two other kinds of assessment, however, that we can say will be common to librarians in all communities. The first kind is a sort of "meta" assessment. How successful are the participatory systems you build and maintain for your community? Do your systems serve all or only 5 percent of your community? How efficient are you in using resources for these participatory systems? Although I don't believe efficiency should be your sole criterion in assessing either your role or the systems themselves, as a professional, you need to be a good, which means also an efficient, steward of the resources at your disposal. And do you and your community agree upon common criteria for assessing the value of services delivered to the community? Is it the level of improvement in economic development? In literacy? In quality of life?

The second kind of assessment that will be common to librarians in all communities could be broadly labeled "critical measures," ongoing examinations of how your library is changing your community's understanding of itself and its institutions. As a librarian, you seek to build systems that empower your community, but, in doing so, you often must prioritize parts of that community. Do you prioritize early reading or adult literacy? If you prioritize literacy of any type, does that mean you devote less time and fewer resources to connectivity? Wanting to bring the Internet into the homes of the disadvantaged, librarians at a public library recently started lending out Internet hot spots. But only members enrolled in literacy and English as a second language courses could borrow the hot spots. In this case, the librarians prioritized those struggling with literacy and connectivity issues over those who were struggling just with connectivity issues.

As a librarian, you must be prepared to critically examine your goals and services. You must understand that, in any community, there are structures of power and privilege, haves and have-nots. To be clear, this is not just a matter of the rich and the poor. If you're a medical librarian, do you answer the doctors' questions before the nurses' or medical students'? Or if you're a bank librarian, do you prioritize the needs of executives over those of the rank and file? All too often, librarians rely either on tradition or on convenience to make these decisions.

The much-needed critical perspective, which looks at library services and systems as a distribution of power, has been increasingly discounted as librarians have moved into the "Information Age." And as library science has become increasingly aligned with the social sciences, many of us have adopted the language of science and have embraced the misguided notion that scientific or rational objectivity should solely define librarianship. To remind yourself just how misguided that notion is, you may want to reread chapter 4 on knowledge creation.

9   Pragmatic Utopians

Core Chapter Concept: Librarians seek to empower the powerless and give voice to the minority.

For some librarians when you strip away the belief of the unbiased librarian you are left with a progressive activist who seeks the toppling of societal regimes of power and control. Some see the discussion of community centrism is a veiled call for Marxist ideals antithetical to the market. For some in the profession this is the radical librarianship that they have long strived for. For others in the profession this as an assured path to destruction of the profession, and a violation of the core value of service.

Some see the librarian as priest, others as activist, still others as civil servant. These views are nothing new. The emergence of the profession itself has been shaped by both progressive and conservative agendas—often at the same time. Andrew Carnegie, a major figure in the creation of libraries of all types, said of his philanthropy:

If I had raised your wages, you would have spent that money by buying a better cut of meat or more drink for your dinner. But what you needed, though you didn't know it, was my libraries and concert halls. And that's what I'm giving to you.[1]

Public libraries did not allow fiction on their shelves, or indeed children on their premises for the better part of the twentieth century because of a belief they imposed upon their communities. Once seen as bastions of social justice, the early public libraries are now seen as enforcing the predominant hegemony of white male privilege.

Here's the thing: communities, like librarians, have their progressives and their conservatives. We must serve all our community members to the best of our abilities. We must make choices every day in line with both our values and our life experiences. You don't give up your humanity, your desires, your passions, or your views when you become a librarian. What you sign on to provide, however, is service that is open and inclusive.

Librarians, in any setting, seek to empower the powerless, and seek to give voice to the minority. We do this because we are part of our communities, and our values and experience tell us there is strength in diversity. Just as we believe that the best decisions come from the richest pool of views, we strive to bring the richest set of voices to bear on our communities' hopes and aspirations.

As librarians, we are pragmatic utopians. We believe that our communities seek a better tomorrow. We are willing to contend with bureaucracy, politics, the uninformed, and the downright hostile for as long as it takes to help our communities reach a better tomorrow in our pluralistic society.

This ideal must also be seen in how librarians, as professionals, treat one another. Our profession is, at its heart, conversation and debate, not unanimity of views, but that debate must be based on respect. Respect for individuals and respect for diversity. Never be afraid to engage in the professional discourse of service, or to share your ideas, no matter how far-fetched or dubious they might seem. Never be afraid to criticize the ideas of others, but always do this as a respectful professional. Librarianship is not about everyone agreeing; it's about everyone working together to find way to improve our communities through knowledge creation.

As a librarian, you'll make mistakes: own them, learn from them, and move on. There's too much work to be done to retreat. As a librarian, you'll take unpopular stances and disagree with the majority and minority alike: make your case, change your stance if you think you should, but always do what you know to be right.

When I first began writing about a community librarianship and a librarian's view of librarianship, there were many doubters. I had (and still have) prolonged arguments with prominent professionals who see libraries as institutions built around a mission primarily of access to collections. Today, that tide has turned, and what you read in these pages may seem like common sense, or natural. This has come about because, as librarians, we have dedicated ourselves to making a difference, not to preserving an institution.

Now let's move on to the next part of our journey and talk about the libraries that librarians build.

Libraries

10 What Is a Library?

Core Chapter Concept: A library is a mandated and facilitated space supported by the community, stewarded by librarians, and dedicated to knowledge creation.

For many years, the following was as close to a definition of a library as I put forth:

I have long contended that a room full of books is simply a closet but that an empty room with a librarian in it is a library.

This simple definition has been widely quoted, but also widely debated. Many feel it discounts the importance of collections, the materials and resources that libraries acquire. Others feel it discounts the power of a library as an institution. Just by working at one of Harvard's libraries, for example, don't librarians gain a bit of prestige from the institution? The point is that many feel that this definition is simply wrong.

I agree.

Even granting the importance of its collection, a library is, of course, much more than a storage place for books and other resources. After all, a bookstore is also filled with books and we don't mistake it for a library, any more than we do a hoarder's overflowing house of magazines and newspapers. But when the *Oxford English Dictionary* defines "library" as "a place set apart to contain books for reading, study, or reference" or "a public institution or establishment charged with the care of a collection of books, and the duty of rendering the books accessible to those who require to use them," it's clear that *action* is at the heart of what a library is. The materials and resources collected there, whether books, periodicals, sheet music, tapes, DVDs, CDs, or anything else, are meant to be *used*—to be read, studied, referred to, played from or with, watched, or listened to.

So the problem with my initial definition is that it says nothing about action. An empty room with a librarian is just a room with a person in it. Librarians have no magical power: they can't transform a room into a place of learning and knowledge creation just by being there. It's only when librarians *act*—when they use a room or a building or an online space to serve their communities that the physical or virtual space becomes a library. So my definition should really read:

I have long contended that a room full of books is simply a closet but that an empty room with a librarian in it *serving his or her community* is a library.

But, even though we've now included the core of librarianship—engagement with our communities—we still need to go a bit further. After all, libraries are far from simply empty rooms or buildings. As institutions, they house and provide access to services, and systems. And, as institutions, their missions can and often do differ from the mission of the librarians who work within them. So we need a more structured and illustrative definition of what a library is.

We already have most of the pieces in place. We know that libraries are systems created or at least actively maintained by librarians with and for their communities. We also know that these systems allow for participation, whether in physical spaces, digital environments, or both. We also know that these participatory spaces or systems are all about knowledge creation and learning. So we can now define a library as

a mandated and facilitated space supported by the community, stewarded by librarians, and dedicated to knowledge creation.

Let's take the key words or phrases of this definition and expand on them.

A Library Is Mandated and Supported by Its Community

Just as, to actually learn, a community member must want to learn, so, to actually have a library, a community must want a library. And, of course, it must not simply declare its desire to have a library; it must make good on that declaration—which means a community must *mandate* and, more important, *support* the library. The mandate can take the form of a charter (most public libraries in the United States, for example), a law (public libraries in the United Kingdom), a budget line (corporate libraries), a box on an organizational chart designated by an accrediting body (many academic libraries at U.S. colleges or universities), or a consensus (the library Occupy Wall Street protesters agreed to create and support for the good of their cause). The support involves dedicating often scarce resources like tax dollars, tuition, or real estate to ensure that the library is not only created but also sustained over time.

People assume that certain types of communities will automatically have libraries. But there are many communities where this is simply not the case. The State of California decided to no longer support libraries in its public schools. And towns across the United Kingdom and the United States have decided not to support their public libraries. In the Netherlands many legal requirements for local public libraries have been eliminated.

The city of Champaign, Illinois had a healthy library. As the city expanded, its residents moved out to the suburbs, forming new towns. These towns chose not to invest in—mandate and support—new libraries because there was already a strong library in the central city. When, however, the expanded service population in the suburban towns began to drain the resources of the central city's library, resources paid for by city taxes, city residents responded by charging the suburban library members a service fee. They made it clear that public libraries aren't free; their members need to pay for them, whether in taxes or in service fees.

A Library Is a Facilitated Space

Although many community members who use a library don't interact directly with librarians, they and other members still benefit from using a space *facilitated* by those librarians, librarians who set the hours of operation; who organize and arrange materials, shelves, tables, and seating; who license online resources; and who create and provide services—all for their benefit. Consider the image in figure 10.1.

Here we can see from how the space was arranged that the emphasis is on individual study, with bookshelves separating the rows of individual study carrels. Compare that to the image in figure 10.2.

Here the materials are arranged on low shelves along the walls of the room, with large, open tables, each seating as many as six members, in the middle. Neither arrangement is accidental; both are facilitated by librarians (no doubt with input from architects, designers, and community members) seeking to promote certain types of conversations and interactions to meet the needs of their communities.

Figure10.1
Yale Law Library

Figure 10.2
Seattle's Nathan Hale High School Library

Figure 10.3
Chattanooga Public Library Home Page

This is also true of digital spaces as well. Look first at the home page for the Chattanooga Public Library in figure 10.3.

What's the emphasis here? Searching the library's catalog is the first option, then a passport service, then row upon row of books. I know the librarians at Chattanooga, and though they provide their community members access to a lot more than books, they chose to highlight books on their home page to facilitate their members' preferences.

Look now at the home page for the Library of Congress in figure 10.4.

Instead of a catalog search panel and displayed resources, we see "Discover" and "Connect." And what have librarians highlighted here? Digital resources and videos, to facilitate the preferences of their far more numerous community members. We'll come back to these well-thought-out decisions, which were made with a lot of community input.

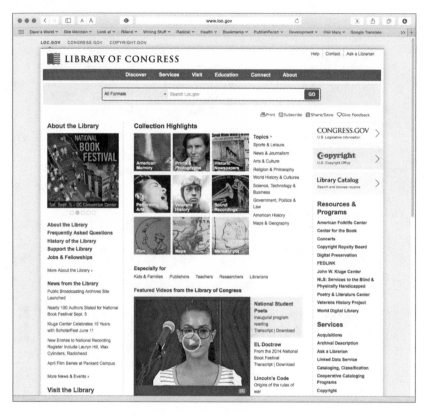

Figure 10.4
Library of Congress Home Page

A Library Is Stewarded by Its Librarians

Libraries are owned by their communities, but they and their assets are *stewarded* by their librarians. These assets can be tax dollars, books and other materials, rare artifacts, physical or virtual space, and trust—the rarest of community assets. To steward these assets, librarians are empowered by their communities to make decisions, to prioritize, and to use their professional skills, experience, and values to maximize their communities' investment.

Take, for example, the case of Miklós Rózsa, a composer who scored many movies, and who won three Oscars for his scores of *Spellbound*, *A Double Life*, and *Ben Hur*. Before his death, Rózsa donated his papers and one of his Oscar statuettes to the Syracuse University Library. People interested in Rózsa's work could now come to Syracuse and examine his letters and original scores. They also could see and even handle his Oscar statuette. When, after many years, the statuette was in need of regilding, the library oversaw and paid for the restoration. As stewards, the Syracuse University librarians had to do more than simply receive and display the materials donated by Rózsa. They had to preserve and restore them, ensure access to them by both their members and the general public, and honor the wishes of the Rózsa estate. To do this, they had to make many decisions based on experience, best practices in the field, and regular consultation with experts at large.

Librarians must constantly adapt and evolve their library systems as their communities evolve. Libraries must constantly reshape themselves as well. As the great Indian librarian S. R. Ranganathan declared in the fifth of his five laws of library science: "The library is a growing organism,"[1] constantly changing and adapting to a changing world.

It's all very well to define what a library is, but who said we needed libraries in the first place? What justifies a community investing in a library? That's the subject of chapter 11.

11 Saving Money and the World

Core Chapter Concept: There are many good reasons for having a library, but all of them involve making a community a better place.

So a library is a mandated and facilitated space supported by the community, stewarded by librarians, and dedicated to knowledge creation. But that doesn't really explain why a community decides to create and support a library in the first place. Yes, there's the "dedicated to knowledge creation" part, but most communities already have systems for knowledge creation: public schools, staff development programs, business intelligence technologies, and so on. Why a library? There are eight core reasons for having a library—to serve as

- a collective buying agent;
- an economic stimulus;
- a center of learning;
- a safety net;
- a steward of cultural heritage;
- a third space;
- a cradle of democracy;
- a symbol of community aspirations.

In truth, rarely is there only one core reason for having a library, and many of the eight have fuzzy boundaries. Nor, of course, do all of the core reasons factor equally in the formation of all libraries. Few corporate libraries were formed to serve as cradles of democracy, for example, although some were. Let's examine the reasons one at a time and see how each applies, if at all, to different types of libraries.

Collective Buying Agent

Stewart Brand famously said, "Information wants to be free." At least, that's what everyone quotes him as saying. The full quote reads:

On the one hand, information wants to be expensive, because it's so valuable. The right information in the right place just changes your life. On the other hand, information wants to be free, because the cost of getting it out is getting lower and lower all the time. So you have these two fighting against each other.[1]

We see the results of this fight everywhere. Books and music are cheaper because their distribution and production costs have been greatly reduced through the use of digital networks. Academics are increasingly putting their papers online for free access, and there is a growing community of people willing to share videos with all sorts of content on free sites like YouTube. But if you take a closer look, "free" isn't quite as "free" as it's cracked up to be. YouTube videos are free to watch—as long as you also watch a few commercials. Business models are changing, but quality information or personalized information still costs real money.

As collective buying agents, libraries have always been one way in which communities pool resources to make big purchases. In university libraries, such purchases are for things like academic journal subscriptions; in public libraries, for popular reading material; in school libraries, for article database subscriptions; and in law offices, for subscriptions to LexisNexis and other legal resource databases like Westlaw. If a resource is too expensive for one community member and that resource is of general interest to the community as a whole, then pooling community assets (taxes, tuition, departmental budgets) to acquire that resource makes sense.

To give you a sense of just how big some of these collective purchases are, consider the following two examples. The following table shows how much it costs the University of Iowa Library to provide faculty, staff, and students online access to academic journals.[2]

Publisher	Number of Journals	Cost to University of Iowa
Elsevier	2,095	$1,641,530
Wiley/Blackwell	1,304	$868,031
Springer	400	$607,540
Sage	608	$243,647
JSTOR	2,319	$97,602
Cambridge University Press	145	$43,940
Project Muse	500	$33,210
Oxford University Press	250	$21,313
Totals	7,651	$3,556,813

It costs this one institution more than $3.5 million a year for electronic access to 7,621 journals, and the library doesn't actually own a single article in any of those journals.

Indeed, database subscriptions cost so much that many libraries pool their resources to purchase them through large consortia like TexShare. Thus the Texas State Library and Archives Commission (TSLAC) found that, as of October 2014, "it would have cost the 645 libraries participating in the TexShare database program $84,158,212 to purchase the database subscriptions that were purchased by the TSLAC for $7,286,620."[3]

There are two requirements that should guide libraries' collective purchases: their librarians need to organize the items purchased, and they need to ensure that the purchases serve the common good. We have spent a fair amount of time on the first requirement: librarians organize the things their libraries acquire by building systems, which include collections and access to networks of expertise as part of their role as facilitators. So let's turn to the second requirement: ensuring that the purchases serve the common good. You'll recall that librarians have service as a core value. This is a value of empowerment for all community members, not just a special few, so that working toward the common good is a natural expression of that core value.

If a community (school, college, town, firm) allocates its money to acquire things, those things should benefit the community as a whole. That may seem obvious, but libraries and communities can miss this point. Let's take the case of a service called "Freegal."[4]

Libraries subscribe to Freegal to allow library members to download music from the Sony music collection as MP3 files. Libraries purchase blocks of downloads (for example, 500 downloads for the community). This sounds like a great service, except that the library (and therefore the community) is paying to allow one library user to download a song for that member's personal use. If another library member wants that song, it will require another download. The libraries (read "the community") paying for the service cannot collect these songs and lend them out or archive them.

Imagine walking into a library, asking for a book, and having the librarian go over to a bookstore to purchase it and then hand it to you to keep. Is this a wise use of community resources? Now imagine using tax funds to build a private road that only one citizen can use. It builds no common resource, brings no economy of scale, and ultimately uses the community pool to enrich select individuals.

To act as a collective buying agent is a nearly universal reason for having a library across all community types. The items collectively purchased have shifted from physical materials (books, periodicals, and such) owned by the community to digital resources (databases, online journals) subscribed to by the community to physical tools (musical instruments, 3-D printers, sewing machines, video production software) owned by the community for community participation and creation.

Economic Stimulus

Related to the collective buying agent role is the idea that libraries of all types stimulate the economy of communities. In Indiana, researchers found that "libraries are a good value. The direct economic benefits that communities receive from libraries are significantly greater than the cost to operate the libraries." Specifically:

• Indiana communities received $2.38 in direct economic benefits for each dollar of cost.
• Public library salaries and expenditures generate an additional $216 million in economic activity in Indiana.
• Academic library salaries and expenditures generate an additional $112 million in economic activity in Indiana.[5]

Studies have found this to be true across a number of states, as seen in the following table:

State, City, or Region	Return on $1 of Investment	Year(s) of Study
Colorado	$4.99	2009[6]
Florida	$6.54	2004[7]
Indiana	$2.38	2007[8]
Pennsylvania	$5.50	2006[9]
South Carolina	$4.48	2005[10]
Vermont	$5.36	2006–2007[11]
Wisconsin	$4.06	2008[12]
Charlotte, NC	$3.15–$4.57	2008–2009[13]
Pittsburgh, PA	$3.05	2006[14]
Saint Louis, MO	$4.40	1999[15]
Southwestern Ohio	$3.81	2006[16]
Suffolk County. NY	$3.93	2005[17]

Where does all the economic stimulus come from? In part, it comes from the fact that libraries are employers whose employees contribute to the local economy through their purchases and taxes. In part, as recent studies show, it comes from the fact that the collective buying of books by libraries actually leads to *more*, not less, book buying by their members.[18] And, in higher education, "libraries are an important consideration when students select a university or college, and, as a result, academic libraries can help institutional admissions boost enrollment."[19]

The economic stimulus of libraries also comes from their helping to create a civic environment that attracts businesses and promotes workforce development. And libraries have played an important role in directly helping job seekers. Indeed, in some libraries, librarians work with entrepreneurs to create altogether new businesses.

Center of Learning

We've already discussed this core reason, at least to some degree. After all, it lies at the core of librarianship and thus also of the libraries and other systems that librarians create. Literacy, learning, and scholarship have always been associated with libraries. In fact, most directors of libraries in the Middle Ages were scholars who also maintained their libraries' collections; this tradition continues today: the Library of Congress was headed by a historian throughout much of the past three decades.

In the early decades of the twentieth century, this reason—that libraries are centers of learning—drove the work of public libraries as the "people's university." Indeed, Melvil Dewey, father of the Dewey Decimal System, believed that public libraries and public schools were "coequal" education institutions.

Today, libraries still have learning at the core of their missions. Summer reading programs encourage a habit of reading, a necessary skill for lifelong learning. School libraries are deeply engaged in literacy instruction, moving from basic reading skills, to research skills, to critical thinking exercises in accordance with their schools' curricula. Even academic and corporate libraries engage in literacy instruction, though they focus on media and social literacy (understanding data visualizations, deciphering trends in social media).

But is it enough to create a resource-rich environment to be a center of learning? Of course not. Simply stockpiling resources does not enhance learning. As a librarian, you must be able to facilitate specific means of knowledge creation in your community for the various age groups and backgrounds of its members. Does your public library work directly with K–12 schools? How does your academic library's collection match the degree programs, courses, and curricula offered at your college? What services do you provide to whom and with what outcome?

Safety Net

When you think of a safety net, you probably think of the poor. To be sure, many libraries provide access to a world of resources and services to those least able to afford it. Public libraries have long brought information to those otherwise unable to acquire it. This is due, in part, to their role as collective buying agents, but, acting as a safety net, today's libraries are also bringing Internet access along with books via bookmobiles to rural community members who would otherwise be denied both. Indeed, a 2008 study showed that three-quarters of public libraries are the only providers of free access to the Internet in their communities.[20]

If you extend this idea of a safety net, libraries are also filling knowledge gaps for their members. School libraries are now lending resources not only to students, but to their parents as well. Academic libraries are offering students classes in the basic research skills they need to get the most out of their courses. Law libraries are helping lawyers and judges alike add vital information literacy to their legal skills. In chapter 16 we'll explore this idea in much greater detail.

Steward of Cultural Heritage

From our discussion in chapter 4, you'll recall that a vital component of knowledge creation is memory and that knowledge is not limited to facts or objective observations. The knowledge of a community includes how it comes to represent itself in the past, present, and future. Historians will tell you that history is not simply an accumulation of dates and events. It is interpretation, interpretation often seen through a current cultural reality.

Take the ancient Library of Alexandria. Many think of it as a huge building filled with the largest collection of scrolls in the ancient world. In this view, scholars from near and far would travel there to study the collected wisdom of the known world. In one often told account, ships coming into the port would be met by city guards, who would confiscate any written materials on board. These would then be taken to the library, where they would be copied, and the copies returned to the ships. Accounts vary widely as to when (48 BC or 270 AD or 391 AD or 642 AD) and by whom (Muslims or Christians or Romans) the library was destroyed.[21]

Largely shaped by how we as a culture define a library, this view of the ancient Library of Alexandria—one immense building with a huge collection of scrolls and other materials—is so pervasive outside of library circles that it is even featured prominently in a Disney World ride.[22] However, the Library of Alexandria was not a single building, but a campus with a number of buildings, the first of which was dedicated to the Muses (from whose name we get the word "museum"). For another, the library was much more like a modern university than a simple repository of documents: scholars from around the known world were paid to take up residence there; the architectural arrangement of its buildings encouraged the scholars to intermingle; when they came up with great ideas, these were written down and added to the library's collection of documents. The librarians of Alexandria, far from being a simple maintainers of documents, were close advisors to the kings and queens of Egypt (who were Greek, by the way). And, finally, the library's destruction, though possibly the result of an invasion or a natural disaster, was more likely the result of a protracted economic decline.

The story of the Library of Alexandria shows us that history is important, but that cultural heritage is more than what is written down, whether in ancient scrolls or modern books and electronic files. It is in the music we listen to, the clothing we wear, the tools we use, and the stories we tell. *Star Wars* is part of our cultural heritage as much as the archetypical young hero myth it's based on. Librarians in libraries of all types play a crucial role in documenting our cultural heritage, but an equally crucial role in preserving and stewarding it as an important memory for our communities and in working with the members of those communities to help them interpret that heritage.

Third Space

Sociologist Ray Oldenburg noted that vibrant communities have three distinctive "spaces": a home space, a work space, and a community—or "third"—space. Although some have extended his idea to include a "fourth" space—for shopping—the main point here is that, to thrive, communities need accessible spaces for their members to come together away from family, away from work—and, yes, away from shopping, too.[23]

Almost all types of libraries serve as third spaces. Public libraries, in particular, are one of the few remaining community-wide spaces for all community members. University libraries have made room for cafés and other gathering places for undergraduates to escape the dorms and classrooms. And school libraries are often seen as safe places for students who don't fit into the world of cliques.

As the use of more and more common spaces is restricted or made to meet other community needs (economic development most notably), library spaces (whether physical or virtual) are becoming increasingly important in bringing community members together.

Cradle of Democracy

Although history tells us you can have libraries without democracy and democracy without libraries, I would argue that in order to have a true liberal democracy, you must have libraries.

The United States is a liberal democracy. So are Canada, France, Germany, India, and Israel. The "liberal" part of "liberal democracy" has nothing to do with a particular political party, or even with how socially progressive a country is; it refers to the belief that democracy is more than voting; it includes constitutional protections of civil liberties and against governmental intrusion. It is the same sense of "liberal" as in "liberal arts education" (which is why to serve as a cradle for democracy is a reason for having a library applies as much to school and academic libraries as it does to public libraries).

Why are libraries so important for a liberal democracy? The short answer is that a true democracy requires the participation of an informed citizenry. The core mission of libraries, public and private, is to create a nation of informed and active citizens.

When library supporters give this reason for having a library, they'll often use one or more of these three quotes:

The people are the only censors of their governors and even their errors will tend to keep these to the true principles of their institution. To punish these errors too severely would be to suppress the only safeguard of the public liberty. The way to prevent these [errors] is to give them full information of their affairs thro' the channel of the public papers, & to contrive that those papers should penetrate the whole mass of the people. The basis of our governments being the opinion of the people, the very first object should be to keep that right; and were it left to me to decide whether we should have a government without newspapers, or newspapers without a government, I should not hesitate a moment to prefer the latter. But I should mean that every man should receive those papers, and be capable of reading them. —Thomas Jefferson[24]

There is not such a cradle of democracy upon the earth as the Free Public Library, this republic of letters, where neither rank, office, nor wealth receives the slightest consideration. —Andrew Carnegie[25]

A popular government without popular information, or the means of acquiring it, is but a Prologue to a Farce or a Tragedy; or perhaps both. Knowledge will forever govern ignorance; and a people who mean to be their own Governors must arm themselves with the power which knowledge gives. —James Madison[26]

Although all three of these quotes share a common message: informed citizens are necessary to sustain a democracy, each emphasizes a different aspect of participating in and maintaining a democracy. Jefferson is talking about transparency, Carnegie about access, and Madison about education. Good libraries take on all three of these aspects. Let's start with transparency.

Democracy and Transparency

In the above quote, Jefferson is clearly talking about newspapers and the press, not libraries. Yet he is also emphasizing the necessity of transparency, which is a goal that librarians and journalists share. To achieve and sustain a functioning representative government of the people, you don't simply vote politicians into office and wait for the next election. There must be oversight of the actions of elected officials to prevent abuse and to shape civic discourse and policy. The abuses of Watergate were not exposed and dealt with through an election, but through investigations and the presentation of documents and evidence of corrupt actions on the part of both elected and appointed government officials.

Libraries further the goal of transparency in a number of ways. Federal government libraries work from within to document, archive, and disseminate the work of federal agencies. For example, if you want to know any law enacted by the U.S. Congress, you can search the Library of Congress's THOMAS database.[27] Or if you'd like to learn about research funded by the National Institutes of Health, you can search the National Library of Medicine's PubMed database.[28]

Nearly 1,250 academic and public libraries around the country further transparency by housing federal government documents as part of the Federal Depository Library Program. If a federal agency prints a report, brochure, form, or regulation, it is deposited at these libraries, which must ensure public access to these materials.

Below the federal level, every state has a publicly accessible law library that houses the laws, regulations, and judicial decisions of that state. Many local libraries store the proceedings of town councils, as well as those of county boards, commissions, and committees and state legislatures. The idea is to allow citizens to inform themselves about the actions of their governments so that they might more knowledgeably and effectively participate in political decision making.

Democracy and Access

What Carnegie talks about in his quote is equal access to the printed record of thoughts—books. Of course, he did more than just talk about it; as a sort of patron saint of public libraries, he built more than 2,500 of them around the world.[29]

Today, libraries of all sorts have extended the idea of access beyond books and other printed materials to the electronic media. Although most clearly seen in the provision of Wi-Fi and public access computers by public libraries, it is also seen in academic libraries granting access to both their printed and their electronic resources not just to faculty and students but also to members of the general public. Thanks to the millions of dollars they spend on statewide database subscriptions, state libraries provide urban, suburban, and rural communities alike with equal access to these resources.

Democracy and Education

Simply having access to the information generated by a working democracy is not enough, as Madison makes plain: "A people who mean to be their own Governors must arm themselves with the power which knowledge gives." Thus you must be able not simply to look up and read a law, whether online or in a printed volume; you must also educate yourself in what the law means and how it might be improved, repealed, or replaced by a better law. The librarians at a good library can help you educate yourself, pointing the way to useful books, articles, videos, and online courses or to local experts willing to explain what you're unclear about.

Democracy and Higher Expectations

Democracy is not an easy thing. Democracy is not neat and tidy. In our daily lives, few of us take the time from our commutes, e-mail, and daily struggles to think about where we fit in the democratic scheme of things. What's more is that in your library you can find the books and the computers, but where is the democracy? Is there an active effort by the librarians to prepare active citizens?

Let me be clear, this is not about being political and ideological. The point is not asking whether your library is lined up with a party or a candidate. Rather, it is asking what difference the library has made in the governance of a community (be it a town, a university, a school, or a corporation). Does your library have a service to inform your local politicians, chancellor, president, CEO, or principal? Shouldn't having a good school library mean that you have a well-informed principal?

Symbol of Community Aspirations

At the most basic level, the library building itself serves as a symbol for a community, the community's desire to be associated with knowledge, and the aspirations of its members for a better life. Their inspiring architecture has made libraries the new cathedrals—a concrete way for communities to make a statement of their importance. San Francisco, Seattle, Salt Lake City, and Vancouver, British Columbia, all have used new library buildings to revitalize their downtowns.

The power of architecture and the statements we seek to make with library buildings in particular can't be denied. Donors to universities want libraries named after them, and architects take great pride in academic libraries, sometimes celebrating the buildings over the library functions themselves.

When it comes to community aspirations, however, we must look beyond the power of a library building to the power of the librarians and services within and, more and more, outside that building not just to inspire but also to encourage and help community members to actually achieve their aspirations. As Barbara Quint, editor of Information Today's *Searcher* magazine, once said, "a library is just what's left over when the librarian goes home, like a coral reef just represents the activity of living coral."[30] It is beautiful and serene but devoid of life, a remnant that can only remind us of a past point in time.

Now more than ever, the future of our communities lies in the decisions and talents of their members, who are the very reason we librarians are all here today. Those members deserve a librarianship that enables radical positive change. The reasons I've just touched on tell us why we have libraries in general. But the real question is, how can we help these reasons become realities in our communities—how can we help our libraries transform themselves to be relevant both now and in the future.

12 A Platform for Knowledge Development

Core Chapter Concept: A library should be a participatory platform that allows a community to share passions, expertise, and resources.

So we have a definition of what a library is and we have reasons for why we have libraries. Now we need to spend some time on how libraries—or, more precisely, how librarians and communities through libraries—do their work.

Libraries have a rich history and a special place in many hearts; indeed, there is an excellent chance that, if you're reading this book, you have a special affinity for libraries. Although I don't mean to diminish either that affinity or the more ethereal qualities of libraries, if you're seeking to be part of them, it does you no good to romanticize their nature. By looking at your library as a system, you gain power to control the work it can do within your community. If, on the other hand, you hold up libraries as near mystical places, rather than focusing on what they could be, and even what they should be, you risk becoming locked into simply perpetuating what they are.[1]

A System of Systems

In chapter 6, I talked about libraries as special participatory systems created and maintained by librarians. Well, in fact, a library is a system of systems. That is to say, the reason we create a library in the first place and the reason we have its librarians work hand in hand to colocate its systems is to gain some economies of scale, as we saw in many of the reasons for having libraries discussed in chapter 11. To avoid the rather awkward phrase "system of systems," I will simply refer to a library as a "platform."

In technical terms, a platform is a set of enabling systems that allows a community to create interconnected functions. Thus a computer is a platform because it allows its users to run many different programs, and its programmers to make these programs without having to do a lot of redundant work (reading information from a disk, displaying things on a screen, mouse clicking, and so on). And a library is a platform because it allows for enabling systems of knowledge creation and facilitation. Some of these systems are well known with long histories, such as item circulation and description, having meetings, and question answering. Some are simply assumed, such as identity management (proving who you are through things like library and ID cards). And some enabling systems are emerging, such as 3-D printing, social networking, and augmented reality.

Here's the thing: even though every library can act as a platform, not every library will have the same set of systems. As we'll see in later chapters, the interface of a library with its community can and should differ radically from one library and its community to the next. But, in each case, the array of systems a library offers should look like its community, not like the librarians who run the platform. Let's start by building a bridge from what many people think are common functions of a library to the idea of a library as a platform and then see how this idea can lead us in sometimes startling new directions.

From Lending to Sharing

Many of you may consider "lending" and "sharing" to be close synonyms, but, in fact, they have very different assumptions and implications. To see how this might be so, think of throwing a dinner party. For a sit-down dinner, you invite guests, calculate the portions you'll need, then buy, prepare, and serve the food to your guests. Everything works out fine unless one or more of your guests decide to bring an additional person to the party. Now you have to either get more food, or reduce the portion size. In effect, each additional person means either greater cost or smaller portions. This is like the lending library model, according to which a library builds a collection of items (books, DVDs) and lends them out. If the demand for any one item grows beyond a certain point, the library must either spend more money (buy more books or DVDs) or ration access (institute waiting lists, curtail loan periods, assess fines).

This is such a common model many of us don't even think about it, let alone seek an alternative. To extend this lending model, rather than increasing their own resources, many libraries have come together in consortia to share scarce resources. This works well, so long as there is slack in the system. But interlibrary loans rarely do work for new best sellers, for example, where every library in the consortium is pressed to meet the demand of its members.

Now, let's go back to that dinner party. This time, rather than hosting a sit-down dinner, you decide to hold a potluck. You provide the space and, say, the drinks, but each guest is asked to bring a dish to share. Now if more people show up, you actually have more food to go around, and normally a greater diversity of food, too. This is like the sharing library model. According to this model, rather than member libraries competing among themselves for scarce resources that must be rationed, the community of libraries itself becomes the resource—or, more precisely, the pool of resources. As it gets bigger, so does the pool of resources.

To take our discussion of the sharing library model one step further, consider the following real-life encounter. A community member (let's call him "George") was talking with Eli Neiburger, associate director of the Ann Arbor District Library: "You know how I can use the catalog to see if my branch has a copy of a book to lend out and, if it doesn't, to see if another branch does?"

"Yes," said Eli, who was in fact in charge of creating that catalog system for Ann Arbor.

"Well," said George, "is there any reason someone couldn't check the catalog to see if *I* had a copy of a book at my home that I'd be willing to share?" George went on to say he was perfectly willing to share his copies of a number of books with other community members who might want to borrow them.

Now, in a lending model, this would make no sense. George's books don't belong to the library, which has no business presiding over his sharing them with other library members. But, in a sharing model, it makes perfect sense. In fact, it made perfect sense to Benjamin Franklin, who is often credited with starting the first public library in America. Except that what he really started was a private subscription library in Philadelphia in 1731. He combined his collection of books and manuscripts with those of other collection holders to make a bigger collection, and then charged library members a subscription fee for upkeep. As more members joined in, the collection grew. It wasn't until Dr. William Pepper created the Free Library of Philadelphia in 1891 that the lending model came to that city.[2]

Now, this raises an obvious point—not every member within a community has the same resources to add to a sharing library, but then not every member needs to share the same resources. And, of course, there'll still be resources too expensive for any one member to afford, and times when pooling resources and rationing make sense. Once you see a library as a platform for sharing resources that can spark knowledge creation, however, you can understand how some communities will want to share beyond books, to expertise, capital, ideas, spaces, software, data, experiences, services, and/or stories. To see what an actual community platform for sharing looks like, let's go to Fayetteville, New York.

What's Your Passion?

Several years ago, librarian Sue Considine realized that she and her colleagues were approaching volunteers at the Fayetteville Free Library all wrong. Like many public and school libraries, Fayetteville's sought out volunteers to help in the functioning of the library. The librarians would have the volunteers help with shelving or checking out books, or with programs like story time. Sue realized, however, that this was exactly the opposite of what should be happening. Rather than having volunteers help the librarians do work, the librarians should be helping the volunteers build the library. She put together a simple form with three questions:

1. What do you love?
2. What are you passionate about?
3. Would you be willing to teach it to or share it with your neighbors?

Community members would be handed this form after every program or service they participated in. Some said they were passionate about reading, others said sewing or home improvement, still others said science fiction or robotics or computers, and on and on.

Sue and the other librarians of Fayetteville would then reach out to these community members to share their passions. They arranged a makerspace with 3-D printers where community engineers could teach other members not only how to print out product prototypes, but also how to do computer-aided design. A community sewing circle came in to share their craft with other community members. One summer, the library arranged with community experts to hold a "Geek Girl" camp to promote science, technology, engineering, and mathematics (STEM) skills in community girls. Librarians had a female fighter pilot come in to talk. They also had community volunteers help build catapults and trebuchets.

In "Human Libraries" at colleges and libraries around the globe, faculty and other community members offer their passion and expertise as "human books" on given topics. One Human Library I was a part of brought in not only faculty, but also local TV producers, lawyers, musicians, meteorologists, and even magicians. Community members could sit and talk with these human books for a half hour or so and get to know what they were about.

The British Library redesigned and retasked its business reading room to be an incubator for entrepreneurs and new businesses. The library sent its librarians for business certification, and also recruited a small army of mentors, lawyers, accountants, and business specialists to be available to budding entrepreneurs. Now community members could come to the business reading room not only for books on business plans, but also for lectures on business, for networking events, where they could pitch ideas to venture capitalists, and for much more.

The point is that all these libraries have become platforms for sharing, not just lending. Librarians have put in place systems that build upon the expertise within their communities. For far too long, people have looked at their libraries as "portals" or "gateways" through which expertise and resources would be brought to their communities from the outside world; libraries provided access (one-way access) to these outside resources with little or no regard for local expertise and knowledge. Now libraries are two-way systems of sharing expertise, knowledge, and resources within and beyond their communities. Now community members can go to their libraries (physically or online) to get inspired to invent or discover, then share their inventions or discoveries with the outside world.

How Can I Help You?

Probably the question most often asked by librarians is "How can I help you?" We ask this of members who come to the reference desk or who call on the phone. We ask it out of a strong desire to serve. But, in reality, it's one of the most arrogant questions we could ask: it assumes that the power to help lies exclusively in our hands: that, as librarians with our expertise, knowledge, and ready access to a host of resources, we are the ones to help our members, who so clearly are in need of assistance.

Imagine if we asked a different question instead—"What are you working on today?" or even better "What's your passion?" This puts power back in the hands of the members being served and invites a conversation where they can more fully describe their situations and any needs they may have. Now there may well be areas where we librarians can help, but this different question leaves ample room for members to express what they already know about the topics of interest to them. It's a question among equals, not one of superiors to supplicants.

Components of the Library Platform

It won't surprise you to read that we've already covered the principal components of the library platform. We did so when we discussed the four ways librarians facilitate: through access, knowledge creation, environment, and motivation.

Access

So libraries provide access to knowledge and resources and to larger conversations for their community members (you'll recall the two-way nature of access). For many libraries and librarian-created systems, this comes down to *description*, *discovery*, and *delivery*.

By way of *description*, librarians describe resources, conversations, and expertise. Generally, this process is called "cataloging" (because the concepts and strategies were developed around entering items into a cataloging system), and the result is metadata (descriptive data or everything you need to know about an item to make a decision to access the item itself). For a long time, traditional cataloging was the pinnacle of access to resources. Skills, techniques, and theories of classification, indexing, abstracting, and controlled vocabularies allowed for an amazing system of access to hundreds of thousands of items in the days of index cards, and even earlier. This body of knowledge has been expanded with the exponential growth of digital information retrieval and automated metadata creation (think Google).

But all the description in the world is irrelevant if not linked to *discovery*. Discovery systems range from something as basic as shelved books for browsing to something as technologically sophisticated as automatic song recognition with your cell phone. I say "basic," but I should say "seemingly basic." Many a company has spent a large sum of money trying to replicate the utility of looking for things shelved properly (think Netflix or Amazon). Discovery services can help you connect to like-minded individuals or needed articles, or they can lead you to unexpected discoveries.[3]

Once members find resources of interest, they need to engage those resources (read them, view them, talk to them, play with them). That is the domain of *delivery*— getting particular resources (books, articles, access to tools) to members. This can be as simple as literally putting an item in the mail (or interoffice delivery), providing a download service for digital items, or, in the "everything old is new again" department, delivery of items housed in closed stacks. But these days, the "closed stacks" are more likely to be items in a robotic bin system offsite, placed there because library collections have outgrown library buildings.

Kimberly Silk, a talented special librarian, loves to point out that Google has solved a huge number of delivery problems by being able to directly access digital items from the web. Still, even when retrieving digital documents, librarians have to do a lot of work to make accessing items from behind a pay wall as easy as possible.

As libraries continue to evolve, delivery will become more and more important, and not only delivery of digital items to community members, but also delivery of member-created items (poems, books, videos, 3-D objects, lectures) to the larger community and outside world. Where librarians have learned the intricacies of licensing resources, they are going to have to dive deep into issues from streaming content, to asserting intellectual property rights on behalf of the creators, not just enforcing laws and contracts on how resources are used.

Knowledge Creation
In the past, the lending library model was all about ensuring that community members had the right to check out, read, or view the items they requested. This put librarians in the unenviable role of copyright cops. They rose to the occasion, however, not only abiding by the law, but also helping to shape it, successfully advocating for exemptions for fair

and educational use. Their experience in doing so will be invaluable as more and more libraries start publishing the works of their community members.

The concept of libraries as publishers, though not new, is being seen in a new light. For centuries, academic libraries have helped scholars author texts and treatises and, selecting certain of these, have published and disseminated them as books. But the academic presses, closely associated with research universities, are now in decline (with a few notable exceptions like the MIT Press); indeed, many have closed their doors. What's taking their place are libraries as open self-publishing platforms.

In the publishing world, a distinction is made between publishers and platforms. Publishers tend to be curatorial shops, selecting what they publish and providing a full suite of services to authors (editing, indexing, design, production, marketing). With the Internet's ascension, digital platforms have made many of the publishers' tools directly available to authors without the curatorial role. From YouTube, which lets almost anyone publish a video, to Medium, which publishes almost anyone's essays, to CreateSpace, which allows almost anyone with Internet access to produce a professionally bound physical volume, these platforms are making traditional publishers feel the heat. Increasingly, community members (scholars, professors, poets, authors) are realizing they can be their own publishers without having to face rejection or accept editorial control by traditional publishing houses.

This transition from publishers to platforms is ideal for libraries in all sorts of communities. Academic libraries are working with faculty to develop open-access journals. School libraries are working with their student bodies to make in-house literary journals. Public libraries are putting in place Espresso Book Machines that will take members' word-processing files and turn them into bound, color-covered volumes in under an hour. Libraries are unleashing the author within us all.

Libraries are not stopping at printed works either. They are helping their members produce videos. and design games and 3-D objects. Several libraries host community gardens, where members learn how to garden by doing—working side by side with community experts.

Why are all these examples considered knowledge creation activities rather than access services? Because, in all of them, members are creating tangible items from the intangible knowledge creation process; they are using these creative technologies to aid memory, spark debate, and reward the creative urge.

Environment

Facilitating through environment, you'll recall, is about creating a sense of physical and intellectual safety. This certainly speaks to the many libraries with buildings. But, just as important, it speaks to the library platforms' stewardship of members' identity information. In controlling what libraries, other library members, and the systems members interact with know about their members, librarians must guarantee member privacy, limiting disclosure to a necessary minimum, while also addressing the issue of protected populations, such as children, and community identity issues, such as gender and race.

This is not as straightforward as you might think. Although many libraries provide members access to e-books, very few of these e-book systems were built by librarians. In fact, many of these systems were not designed with libraries in mind at all. One system provided by Adobe lets library members read e-books on their mobile devices. But the system sends data on who is reading what and when in plain readable text back to corporate headquarters on a regular basis. This means that, if they are unaware of this practice, librarians using the system are inadvertently undermining member privacy. Although the library platform must be as open as possible to accommodate innovative ideas and tools from many industries, librarians must ensure a principled playing field that is biased toward member needs and concerns.

Does that mean that libraries should not offer e-books? No. Does it mean that tools like Adobe Reader should be automatically excluded? No. It does mean, however, that just as librarians facilitate learning conversations among members, they must facilitate an ongoing dialogue in the library itself. True to their core values in offering services and technologies to their members, librarians must be sure to discuss with them the consequences and trade-offs involved.

Motivation

Summer reading programs in public libraries give out prizes to promote literacy; academic libraries turn student orientation into role-playing games. And new concepts in gamification and badging look to turn even the most routine tasks into external motivation machines—new means of rewarding community members for their learning and participation. But not all means of motivation have to be external.

Take the Pine Grove Middle School in Syracuse, New York, and the iStaff program there. School librarian Sue Kowalski started the program small, assembling a group of student volunteers to help around the library. But, unlike the Fayetteville approach of letting volunteers share their passions with other community members, Sue built upon the volunteers' inner motivation by delegating more and more of her job to them and by helping them both learn and develop a sense of ownership in the library through their new responsibilities. As the program grew, students went from simply shelving materials to organizing them and from arranging chairs for teachers' classes to giving classes to teachers on new technologies and library resources. Some of Sue's iStaff team members would work for only five or ten minutes a day, but if they were going to be late, they'd have their parents call Sue to let her know. They were invested in the success of the library program because Sue had invested in *their* success (for more on Sue's program, see her contribution, "iStaff," in chapter 15).

As librarians, we must create a sense of ownership in our libraries by our community members. This is more than members paying taxes or tuition; this is the belief that the success of our members and the success of our libraries are joined. Faculty should feel that they do better research because of our libraries. Lawyers should feel they are better at the practice of law because they are a part of our libraries. This sense of ownership arises for two reasons. The first is that the benefits of our libraries to our members are defined in the members' terms, not in the libraries' (it's not about the number of times they visit our libraries, it's about how well they do their jobs because they visited the libraries). The second is that we and our community members work together in making decisions on our library platforms and services.

13   Fitting Knowledge in a Box

Core Chapter Concept: Reducing libraries, librarians, and their tools to a universal scheme is impossible—and dangerous.

And so we've come to the point where many discussions of libraries start: types of libraries and how libraries are organized. There is a reason we come to these topics so late in this guide. The strong focus of librarians on how libraries are categorized is a huge problem because it implies that the structure and mission of libraries are determined more by the types of communities they serve than by the communities themselves (believing that an academic libraries have more in common with one another than a small community college library might have with a school library, for example). It also implies that there is some overriding universal structure common to all libraries Both of these implications are, in fact, misconceptions born of an overemphasis on efficiency in libraries over the past 200 years and an adherence to reductionism as a way of approaching the world.

Daedalus's Maze

A joke to start out. God calls a meeting in heaven and invites Carl Linnaeus, the father of modern taxonomy (he's the reason we use Latin names to label plants), Melvil Dewey, who created the Dewey Decimal System, and Betty Johnson, a rural library director who had died the previous week in a car crash (it wasn't her fault).

God says, "Well, I've done it. I've announced the Day of Judgment is upon us. But I have a problem. Turns out when I first came up with this plan there were fewer than 7,000 of you, but today there are more than 7 billion. They're all behind that door over there, and I'm having a hard time figuring out who gets to go to heaven and who gets to go to hell. You are all experts in classification, so I thought you could help out."

"No problem," says Linnaeus, as he steps through the door. An hour passes, two, three. After four hours, a haggard Linnaeus trudges out the door, muttering to himself, "So many people, I ran out of Latin."

"I shall not fail," declares Dewey, confidently striding through the door. Seven hours later, a desperate Dewey crawls back: "I ran out of numbers!"

Without a word, Betty Johnson goes through the door and emerges half a minute later: "Done!"

"That's astounding!" says God. "How did you do it?"

"Simple," says Betty. "I asked all those who ever voted to support a library budget to raise their hand, and told the rest they could go to hell."

Betty's "solution" is the epitome of efficiency through reductionism, the idea that you can understand any complex system by breaking it into smaller and smaller parts and that, once you understand all the parts (or, in Betty's case, the most important part), you'll understand the whole. It is with this view that Dewey put forth his decimal classification system. He took the world's knowledge (defined at the time primarily as nonfiction books and manuscripts) and broke it down into smaller and smaller parts until he described everything, or thought he did. Dewey fit the world's knowledge into ten major categories from "General Works" (the 000s) to "History and Geography" (the 900s). Then he broke these ten categories down into subcategories and kept breaking these down until he could "correctly" identify a single item. Let's use "Religion" (the 200s) as an example. Dewey broke "Religion" into ten subcategories, one for religion generally (the 200–209s), one for the philosophy and history of religion (the 210s), one for the Bible (the 220s), six for Christianity (the 230s through 280s), and one subcategory for "Other Religions" (the 290s), under which he grouped Islam with Babism and the Baha'i faith (in the 297s), and then he kept on breaking these down until he ended up assigning one number to the King James Bible (220.52) and another to the Koran (297.122).

To be clear, despite my potshots at the classification approach, I readily admit that it's been amazingly powerful and successful over time. Indeed, throughout history, libraries have used the power of classification—specifically, reductionist classification—to great effect. Their classification systems have brought order and accessibility to millions upon millions of items. And they allowed libraries throughout the nineteenth and twentieth centuries to gain extraordinary efficiencies that saved the time of community members, cut costs, and gave birth to the very profession of librarianship. In an analog world, these systems still rule.

The problem with the classification approach in librarianship today is twofold. First, too many librarians feel that there is such a thing as an "objective" classification system (we addressed this in chapter 4, so I won't rehash it here). And, second, too many librarians have sought to bring the "efficiencies" of classification to our profession itself. Take a look at a library organization like the American Library Association (ALA, which counts Dewey among its founders). The ALA is first subdivided into the Public Library Association, the Association of College and Research Libraries, and the American Association of School Librarians (the only unit that has "librarians" in its name), and each of these subdivisions is further subdivided into a myriad of committees and task forces. The urge to subdivide has led librarians to slot themselves into ever smaller groups to get work done. "I'm not a librarian; I'm an academic librarian"; "I'm not an academic librarian; I'm a technical services academic librarian"; and so on. It has become a sort of Daedalus' Maze—a system so complex it is inescapable.

All this subdividing makes it difficult to approach the field in a holistic manner. For example, there was an impassioned debate about information literacy among academic librarians.[1] They debated things like threshold concepts and the importance of having or not having standards. It was an intense and important discussion, but one that occurred totally outside another impassioned debate about information literacy among school librarians over the past two decades. The result is that these two groups of librarians failed to benefit from each other's insights and perspectives on a key issue for both. Thus, in their quest to capture the efficiency of classification tools, librarians have actually fragmented both their work and their effectiveness.

This same quest for efficiencies through universals can be seen in the way many libraries structure themselves. Most library staffs of any size are divided into administration, public services, and technical services. The public service division manages community-facing systems (except the catalog) such as reference, circulation, story times, in-depth research services, and so on. The technical service division manages collection development, cataloging, and computer systems including the catalog. In fact, it is the catalog that shows the limitations of this approach even to the most die-hard traditionalists. On the one hand, the catalog is an inventory system. Technical service librarians use it to collect and catalog materials. On the other hand, the catalog forms the community-facing interface with that collection. Members can use the catalog to find and evaluate items and, in many online systems, to leave reviews and even to add their own materials or resources.

Having public service and technical service divisions may make sense to librarians, but these divisions are not based on how community members interact with library systems. When, say, scholars in an academic or public library or in an industrial research lab work with librarians to find out what is already known about the topics of their studies, they go to public services. And when they want to safely store the data they've gathered, they go to technical services. But what if they also want to set up blogs to disseminate their findings or to incorporate them in online courses? Do they go to public or technical services? So we see how a relatively well known community type, scholars, must dance back and forth between divisions created by and for librarians. How do inventors using 3-D printing or genealogy researchers publishing books map to how librarians organize themselves? The short answer is they don't.

You may think this is more a rhetorical or logical problem than a practical one. Yet it lies at the heart of how community members interface with the systems of the library. It is the same problem that has led to public libraries in Syracuse, New York, looking exactly like those in Seattle, or Norway, or Kenya. It's a "McDonald's approach" to libraries. Make libraries all the same the world over so that members will find them familiar no matter where they go. Except that librarians and the libraries they build are not in the fast-food business; they're in the community and knowledge creation business. Libraries need to look like their communities.

Should librarians be organized into technical and public service divisions simply because "that's how we've always done it," or "that's the most efficient way" (efficient to the librarians, not the community)? The answer should be self-evident: the best way to organize the professionals and staff of libraries is to meet the unique needs of their communities.

Thus one academic library replaced technical and public services with teaching and research services, and one public library turned all of its librarians into production librarians to help community members create knowledge, and videos, and books, and websites. We've already talked about how the British Library transformed reference librarians into business consultants. The point is that communities shouldn't have to conform to a rigid library structure just so it's easy for librarians to find their cohorts in the field. Each library should look like its community. Our job as librarians is to find great ideas in any industry or structure and adapt them for our local conditions. So let's stop reducing ourselves, our libraries, and our communities to some common denominator that mangles the unique qualities all three of these bring to the task of knowledge creation.

With the very real consequences of reduction laid out, I shall now turn to ways in which different types of libraries can embrace their communities. The goal is not to create a common template for academic, public, school, and special libraries—quite the opposite. The goal is to highlight examples and means of shaping the library platform for overarching communities.

Core Chapter Concept: Academic libraries proactively speed the scholarly conversation.

Part of, or aligned with, institutions of higher education, academic libraries tend to acquire comprehensive collections, do little weeding of them over time, and seek to accelerate the pace of scholarly dialogue in research and teaching.

These libraries are already part of a culture and community dedicated to learning and founded on the principles of knowledge creation through conversation. Textbooks, journals, symposia, and lectures are all conversations. They may be sequential, rigid in format, or plodding, but they are conversations nonetheless. Peer review is a form of discipline-based conversation about what is acceptable and what is not. The recent adoption of web-based scholarly publishing channels (institutional repositories, open-access journals, and academic social networks) by many disciplines shows a resurgence of the conversational aspects of scholarly publishing and the alignment of librarianship to the larger mission of a college or university.

Still, many more colleges and universities are devoted to teaching than to research. Here again, academic librarians are well positioned to highlight the shared mission of knowledge creation and learning to their faculty members. As pressure increases in all forms of university-level teaching to adopt more participatory forms of learning, academic librarians have a great opportunity to lead the way.

The proposed academic library activities that follow will not all be appropriate for every academic library. That's because academic libraries, like all libraries, must shape themselves and their services to the specific communities they serve.

A Library with an Integrated Research and Development Agenda

A college is an institution of discovery. From physics, to religion, to mechanical engineering, the academy seeks to push the bounds of what we know and how we do things. An academic library is no different.

Academic librarians and staff should engage in an active research agenda and seek resources and leadership around the issues of scholarly publishing, information literacy, preservation of records and metadata, and how knowledge creation and information shape higher education and society. I was once a part of a conversation on the future of scholarly publishing at an academic library. The assembled faculty and librarians went through a litany of new platforms for the dissemination of new knowledge: blogs, open-access journals, video, digital preprints, apps, and so on. At the end of considerable discussion, one librarian remarked, "We at the library are waiting to see what the faculty choose in terms of scholarly output so we can support it."

Relying on faculty immersed in their disciplines and research to imagine new forms of scholarly communications is, at best, optimistic. What's needed to lead the way to these new forms is a cross-disciplinary set of experts on scholarly records and impact dedicated to the invention and implementation of new and better means of knowledge dissemination. What's needed are librarians who can shift from being caretakers to being curators, and from being curators to being activists.

Not only should academic librarians engage in these conversations; they should also actively seek grants to support their work. They should host visiting scholars and postdoctoral positions from across the globe; they should build a coherent research agenda in advancing and speeding scholarly discourse and discovery. Academic libraries should become the places to watch on matters of scholarly metrics, knowledge dissemination platforms, and the use of digital networks for scholarly collaboration.

Integrating Students across the Campus in Library Service

Students in different disciplines can gain invaluable real-world experience applying their classroom learning to real problems in a fully functioning academic library. Students should work shoulder to shoulder with academic librarians in exploring how what they learn in the classroom can change industries and disciplines.

Learning theory and advances in instruction have shown us the importance of fusing research and practice. Although the ideal courses are combinations of practica and symposia, where can university students get access to real problems—particularly, the most meaningful problems that cut across the boundaries of classes, colleges, and disciplines? The short answer can be the academic library.

Through internships, independent studies, work-study, hourly positions, and class projects, students can work with librarians on production teams. A scholar needs a website? The production team takes control. Not only does the team produce code (computer science students), images (illustration students), designs (design students), and such, but the team's librarians (information technology services and home departments) ensure that projects meet quality standards and can be sustained and preserved over time. Students learn, faculty excel, librarians facilitate, and authentic, measurable learning takes place.

The Library Serves as a Hub for New Forms of Instruction

Academic librarians should play a unique role in spanning disciplinary boundaries to identify, understand, and disseminate innovative educational models. These include massive open online courses (MOOCs); continuous education; alumni teaching; intensive programs to improve science, technology, engineering, and mathematics (STEM) education; the flipped classroom, online education, and hybrid courses.

Just as the academic library's mission of speeding the scholarly conversation creates a natural research agenda for its librarians, so, too, does it make the academic library into an ideal incubator of instructional experimentation. By understanding new methods of instruction online and in person (and most often in hybrid settings), academic librarians should advance their own curriculum of information literacy. They can also serve as valuable partners with faculty and college technology services in areas such as distance education.

That said, the real potential for library-based instructional innovation lies in continuous education. Rather than looking at the university as a sort of commencement provider (starting people in careers with education at the bachelor's level, adding management and depth at the master's level, or depth and research skills at the doctoral level), what if the university was able, after educating people to whatever degree level they wished, to sustain them throughout their life with continuous education through access to faculty, graduate students, staff, and other alums? Imagine a knowledge hub where alumni and others regularly interact with their college to increase their skills, certify new learning, and teach the next generation of students.

Across colleges and universities, faculty are struggling with new modes of instruction. From the flipped classroom to online education, these efforts need to be brought together. Creating a hub for this innovation allows the academic library to adequately support new forms of instruction, but, more important, it speeds diffusion of innovative practices to all corners of the campus. The world of higher education is rapidly changing, and colleges and universities are ripe for disruptive change. Rather than wait for this to happen, they should foster it to force other institutions to respond.

Reinventing the University Press as a Community Publisher

University presses used to be selective imprints—focused on a thin slice of a university's scholarship. This system worked well when there were a lot of academic presses. As the number of these outlets has decreased or consolidated, what is left is a disconnected series of islands.

Imagine a new library-owned university press that worked directly with faculty across all the disciplines to develop new forms of publishing. This new university press could produce apps, courseware, and podcasts in addition to monographs. It could be an innovator in self-publishing and in developing new platforms to turn scholarship into action and benefit for society.

Academic librarians can create a fertile field of scholarship and instruction by creating a robust platform for scholars, instructors, students, and staff to disseminate their ideas, and engage the larger domains and society in conversations. But this platform must not simply move from printing books to producing e-books; it must also dip deeply into the academic ferment that precedes studies and publications. It must provide a forum for sharing, discussing, and refining new ideas for grants. It must provide a mechanism to gather, store, and share the data and insights of funded research. And it must both archive finished projects and continuously relate them to new efforts, building a long, clear map of progress and success.

The new library-owned university press is a community publisher. Managing and maintaining the community's illustrations, lectures, books, data sets, this publisher can take the most exciting part of scholarship—the debates and investigations—and make it accessible to the world. But it must not only publish academic articles; it must also marry them to a forum, and courseware, and ongoing research.

Making Tenure Decisions More Informed

Because tenure is one of the most expensive and long-lasting commitments a college or university can make, it should be granted making use of the best information. Academic libraries can assign librarians to all faculty members being considered for tenure in any given year. These academic librarians can provide intensive citation analysis of the members' works, using the latest in new and alternative metrics to measure impact. This service can provide all involved in the tenure decision with objective and in-depth data. A natural extension of an agenda in scholarly communication, a robust university publisher, and librarians embedded in research is the ability to tell a more accurate and compelling story of a university's scholarly achievement. By tasking academic librarians with upcoming tenure cases, the university can directly inject real measures of impact and best practices into the tenure and promotion process.

There are other benefits of tying academic librarians into the tenure process. They can create a real and up-to-date inventory of the academy's scholarly output. In learning more about the work of faculty, they can find better ways to support this work. A university's preprint archives can move from serving as a simple document repository to becoming a living open-access journal available to the world, one that highlights the strength of the university's research to other institutions.

Gone are the days when academic libraries were simply repositories of books and other materials, set off to the side and not actively serving the missions of their universities. What's needed today is a commitment by university administrators, faculty, students, and librarians to reinvent the whole concept of academic libraries.

To be sure, the transformation of academic libraries won't happen overnight, nor are all academic librarians ready to carry out this transformation.

They need motivation, support, and a vision to drive them forward; they need continuous training and a culture of innovation and exploration.

I've seen some impressive academic libraries in my time, from those with soaring ceilings and Gothic vaults to those with brutalist towers full of rare treasures, and from those with walls of marble to whole edifices of steel. An academic library can make you feel both smart and unworthy in a way that spurs you on in your quest for knowledge. But the most impressive of all these libraries are the ones that are filled with students and scholars working with their librarians.

In the Syracuse University Library, you'll find cuneiform tablets thousands of years old but they'll last thousands more because the library worked with faculty in the College of Visual and Performing Arts to fire the clay tablets into stone. What makes this and other academic libraries great, however, is not the age of the materials in their collections, but their dedication to learning. They see the missions of preservation, access, and inspiration as joined; indeed, they believe that the value of an original sixteenth-century manuscript lies in how much it can inspire, not in how much it would bring at auction.

Academic libraries were once the province solely of scholars and the elite few. As a college education has become ever more important in today's society, the barriers of gender, race, and class have been broken down. Academic libraries and the librarians who run them need to be in the vanguard of this expanding access to higher education and to the scholarship and knowledge that make it possible. They must help guide the academy in providing not only sources for scholarship, but scholarship itself to the world.

15 School Libraries

Core Chapter Concept: School libraries can be places of learning and empowerment, but only by sharing ownership with their students.

Just as academic libraries are aligned with the educational missions of their parent institutions, so, too, are school libraries. They are places of learning in a place of learning. In fact, many school librarians have long ago adopted the spirit and techniques of learning that are presented here—but far from all. I was recently on a tour of a secondary school. Part of the tour was a stop in the library. I asked the librarian how the library functioned in the school, for example, did students have scheduled time in the library.

"No, this is not an elementary library," she said.

"Do you have a curriculum that you work with?" I asked.

"What do you mean?" asked the librarian.

"For example, do you teach information literacy?"

The librarian looked at me blankly.

"Actually, we do that in the English classes," a teacher who happened to be grading papers at a nearby table (in the mostly empty library) chimed in. "It's a big part of what we teach. We even teach media literacy in the computer labs."

For the next fifteen minutes, the teacher outlined an information literacy curriculum and how it was integrated not just in English classes, but across the classes for many other courses as well, while the librarian stood by saying nothing. The English teacher ended her overview with "I love libraries."

All I could think is that she must love libraries if she could turn a blind eye to a school librarian so unequipped to talk about libraries. I'm all for teachers being advocates for school libraries and able to describe library activities, but the teachers at this school had put their information literacy curriculum into place *without* the librarian. The school library was a place to send students for resources only. It reminded me of the overwhelming number of studies that show that the presence of an active school library program with a certified school librarian improves student performance. But "active" is the operative word here. Having a room and books and calling it a "library" does not equate to improved performance of students.

Active school librarians, normally one per library, or sometimes shared across a school district, work with students and teachers to both enhance existing learning outcomes and implement a curriculum of information literacy. When they do their work well, they build participatory opportunities for students to take ownership of their learning, opportunities which are hard to come by outside of the library due to the increasingly structured curricula of their classes.

What follows is an example of an outstanding school librarian empowering her students through ownership in their library and in their learning. Sue Kowalski is the school librarian at Pine Grove Middle School in Syracuse, New York. She has built an award-winning program that is all about students and participation.

---

iStaff
by Sue Kowalski

When I first started working as a school librarian at Pine Grove Middle School in East Syracuse Minoa School District, I was thrilled to have so many students who wanted to "help" during their nonacademic times in school. I enthusiastically found tasks that kept them busy. Word spread that I loved "little helpers," and soon many were sent my way for various reasons. Managing these volunteers was becoming a full-time job, and, even though the tasks were quite simple (straighten chairs, dust, straighten books, sharpen pencils), I sensed they wouldn't get done unless I was involved. At first, I thought about sending out a big "Thanks, but no thanks." But then I realized that the problem was not with my helpers, whose energy was positive, even priceless, but with my approach to them, which was much in need of revision.

I had to up the stakes, provide structure, and look to the limitless possibilities of having a vibrant student volunteer program. So I gathered together a few students to brainstorm moving things forward. We decided the program should be only for students who *wanted* to be a part of it, that it should be regarded as a privilege, and that there should be expectations for those involved. My student brainstormers were very focused on rules and violations, but I steered them toward bigger concepts. We named our program "iStaff," created guidelines, and designed a brief application. Next came the marketing, outreach, and training. I saw immediately the need to transfer authority and guidance of the program to student managers, who would handle applications, passes, lists of tasks and jobs, and training.

Fast-forward a few years: iStaff is now part of our school district culture. There are iStaff teams working through the library at the middle school and also at some elementary schools. iStaff has become synonymous with leadership, problem solving, advocacy, and teamwork. It is even built into our District Strategic Plan. Our teams are called on to finish projects, come up with solutions, and manage work flow. Now, instead of creating lists of tasks, jobs, and guidelines for work to be done, our focus is on innovative solutions to problems affecting our library, schools, and community.

With the students' increased responsibility has come their increased respect for the roles they are performing. Yes, there are always functional tasks to manage like circulation, deliveries, distributing promotional materials and other administrative business. But, the difference now is that the students are helping coordinate what needs to be done. Instead of my telling them, "Make a sign for sixth graders that says this," for example, we work together to create something to catch the attention of those sixth graders. Rather than my telling them, "These are the programs we will host in the library this year," I pass the torch to them: "Come up with a calendar of programs we should have this year and make them happen." And instead of having them deliver technology to a classroom, I put iStaff in the role of actually providing instruction. iStaff students have taken the lead with classes in coding, in creating and running an e-newspaper, in EasyBib, in digital presentation tools, and in the use of apps and websites.

Having a quality collection makes good sense for a school library. Having a quality collection that represents student voices makes even better sense. iStaff students get more connected with what we have, what we need, and what students are asking for when they handle circulation, displays, shelving, and deliveries. I seldom order anything that students haven't suggested. Certainly, I point out new titles, reviews, and subject areas for them to consider, but their leadership drives what we purchase.

Pre-iStaff, I would have created a webpage, Libguide, Symbaloo, or something similar and asked students to *test* things for me. Now I provide a framework, learning goal, and parameters and turn the job over to them. For example, instead of asking iStaff students to test a link to a Symbaloo about

Earth Day that a teacher has requested, I connect the students to the tool, tell them what we need and turn them loose.

Our iStaff teams have become the biggest advocates for our library program. They are our voices, our eyes, our perspective, our reality. I no longer have to seek out students to advocate for the library program. It has become part of what they do and it's contagious. iStaff students are in classes, on teams, in clubs, and involved in our community. They share with their parents and spread the word about what they're doing, how they're leading, and what impact this is having. Every year, I take a group of iStaff students to Legislative Day for Libraries in Albany. Though we review general expectations on protocols and such for the day, I seldom suggest what the students should talk about regarding the value of the school library. I'm confident they know that what the library brings to their world is not only personal, but rich with perspective based on their leadership role and active involvement.

iStaff students participate in board meetings, special events, daily management, instruction, and technology initiatives, working in and through the library as the leadership opportunities require. Our goal is that students will step up in a leadership role as needed. To that end, we want to empower them with the skills and confidence to become assertive, demonstrate initiative, communicate effectively, and exemplify creative problem solving, qualities that will serve them well in later life.

Strong libraries need the engagement of their communities to thrive. The iStaff program is worth every investment of time and energy needed to make it work. We worry less about the little things and more about how we can shoot for the stars and increase our impact. Our biggest challenge is getting as many on iStaff as want to be. We will continue to assess, revise, and expand our program to connect all interested students to authentic leadership opportunities in our school community.

iStaff Takeaways

Looking at volunteers as assets to achieve both community and library functions ("I seldom order anything that students haven't suggested"), Sue has indeed created an expansive community for her school. iStaff students not only work and add content, but even advocate on behalf of the library.

Sue is still doing instruction, collection and curriculum development, and tech support, but she is no longer the only person in the library doing these. Students and teachers are now helping her. Sue's story doesn't have to stop at her school's edge. This is how other one-librarian and other small libraries can embrace the community approach. Indeed, we can imagine an iStaff for a town or a college. All too often, we get stuck where Sue began her story—we see working with the community as a burden (it takes too much time to organize volunteers). Yet when we librarians truly embrace the power and abilities of our community members—be they eleven-year-olds or hundred-year-olds—we find we receive so much more than we could ever expect.

The Future of School Libraries

The unfortunate reality of school library programs throughout the world is that they're being closed. Although sometimes this means the libraries themselves are also being closed, more often than not, the libraries remain open, but their trained school librarians are replaced by teachers or volunteers unequipped to push forward a curriculum or agenda for change. In some countries, school libraries are staffed by teachers unable to handle the stress of the classroom. This is unfortunate indeed, especially in light of the well-documented benefits of active school libraries. In revisiting librarians' means of facilitation, let me suggest what active school libraries might look like.

Access

Access to knowledge and materials is an important part of learning, and therefore an important part of school libraries. These days, that access to materials is increasingly online. Databases, study tools, and digital resources of all sorts are finding their way onto the pages of school library websites.[1] These online tools mean that students can use library resources anytime from anywhere.

Such access can have unintended consequences though. In 2009, Cushing Academy, a private boarding school in Massachusetts, eliminated nearly all of its physical nonfiction collection. Rather than a way of minimizing the school library (as it was portrayed in the popular media),[2] it was a way to modernize the library's collection by replacing the out-of-date physical nonfiction resources with digital equivalents. It was also a way to free up space for instruction and study.

It had the unintended consequence of increasing demand for school librarians. Now that students could get to resources at all hours of the day, they wanted access to librarians beyond the school day as well. Note, however, it wasn't simply that students needed tech support after hours; they had come to rely on the guidance and instruction of school librarians.

This leads to two other aspects of access in active school libraries. The first is their providing student members with access to people, not just things. This includes adding Skype talks with authors to their collections and creating school-wide and indeed cross-school projects where students team with local experts in science, history, and the arts and with students in other schools in the United States and around the globe on authentic research projects. The second aspect is their serving as a platform for publishing the works and ideas of student members to the outside world, whether by hosting podcasts and videocasts[3] or by the actual publication of student reports on topics such as local history.

Too many school librarians see the Internet as a vast disorganized pile of resources to be categorized and listed. For them, modern access is cobbling together web guides and online links for teachers to use. For the truly gifted school librarians, however, the Internet is a chance for knowledge amplification, community building, and authentic learning. In the words of Buffy Hamilton, the "Unquiet Librarian": "By establishing a climate of participation, risk-taking, acceptance of 'messy' learning, and inquiry, we can create conversations that in turn create school libraries that are responsive and organic. A participatory approach to librarianship can ultimately lead to learning experiences that, in the words of Steve Jobs, 'make a dent in someone's universe.'"[4]

Knowledge Creation

When speaking of knowledge creation in the school library, Buffy goes beyond simply pointing to resources; she partners directly with teachers to engage students on assignments. In her "Write-Around Text on Text" sessions,[5] she actively facilitates the students' learning and knowledge creation: students sit together around a table to annotate a common text (usually a passage from a book they are reading), learning from conversation and direct participation rather than from being taught in a class.

The power of school libraries and learning comes not from maintaining a collection of books or from turning the school library into another classroom with a top-down curriculum. It comes from building a rich playground of resources, people, and activities and from empowering students to create.

Environment

If you're building a school library in Texas for a school with more than 2,000 students, you need a school library of at least 7,500 square feet—at least according to the Texas State Library and Archives Commission (TSLAC).[6] Though I would never want to argue with an organization as powerful and prestigious as TSLAC, you can have a great school library even in an RV. The key lies in the environment you create in the library's real and virtual spaces.

That environment needs to be not only safe but also engaging. More than simply refuges from bullying and the pressures of a testing culture or spaces to be quiet for students, school libraries should be places where students are both welcomed and engaged by school librarians and staff who understand their needs and who actively facilitate their learning.

I've seen school libraries with no books, ones housing hydroponics experiments, others colocated with school counseling, and still others that were more computer labs than conventional libraries. I've yet to find one format that guarantees success. Yet all successful school libraries do have one thing in common: people who care for the *whole* student.

Motivation

Caring for the whole student might be a nice lead-in to talking about the motivation of students, but I would rather talk about the motivation of teachers. Too many teachers include a "library component" in their lessons that is little more than looking something up in an encyclopedia. But great school library programs motivate teachers to be better instructors.

Magic happens when classroom teachers partner with teacher-librarians. Simple "Look it up" or "Read the following" assignments can be transformed into exercises in critical thinking. School librarians can work with classroom teachers to develop lessons that span the information literacy spectrum, from finding materials to combining them in coherent wholes. Better assignments lead to more motivated students, better learning, happier teachers, and better school libraries.

Core Chapter Concept: The community is the collection.

Funded by public dollars at the city, regional, or national level, public libraries in many countries are open to serve the general public of their localities.[1] Their broad mission—broad because the communities they serve are broad—can be summed up as "community improvement." In many municipalities, the public library is the only civic organization tasked to provide direct service to citizens of all ages, all socioeconomic groups, and all vocations. Some public libraries are direct departments of larger governing bodies, but many act as semi-independent organizations with their own oversight (normally in the form of a citizen board), and even their own tax structure.

As with academic libraries, public libraries can be small, like a rural library with a part-time librarian serving a community in the hundreds, or large, like the Queens Public Library in New York City with a service population in the millions. Yet big or small, municipal or regional, all public libraries have to prove their value, how they have used the public resources allotted them (tax dollars, space) to improve their communities.

For centuries, public libraries leaned heavily on the basic reasons put forth for having libraries in general. Public libraries have provided economic benefit, reduced costs for the acquired resources, and worked to promote literacy (typically limited to reading readiness). But it is worth looking at how public libraries of all sizes can modernize their classic functions of reference (answering the questions of their community members) and collection development (building, organizing, and maintaining tools for their members to use in knowledge development).

Community Reference

The term "community reference" was first put forward by Jamie LaRue, former director of the Douglas County Public Library in Colorado. LaRue sent his librarians out of the library to be part of important community organizations such as Chambers of Commerce or Arts Councils. He gave these embedded librarians three tasks: show up, pay attention, and stay in touch.[2]

Associate Director for Public Services at Salt Lake County Library Peter Bromberg was given the task of implementing the community reference model for Salt Lake. His librarians were unsure about the value of doing community reference and unclear about how it differed from traditional outreach or even marketing. For many of them, leaving the library to pro- actively engage community members in nonlibrary spaces was outside their comfort zone and, indeed, beyond their conception of what "library work" entailed.

During a series of meetings with the librarians, where Peter listened to their concerns, he explained the service in a way that resonated with many of them:

When you go into the community you're really doing two things: reference, and collection development. In reference what do you do at the desk? You listen, ask questions, and once you have a clear sense of how someone's question can be answered, you connect them to the best resources. When doing community refer- ence, we're using the same skills and behaviors, but we're doing it in their space, not at our reference desk.

So when we're at an Arts Council or Chamber of Commerce meeting, we listen and ask open-ended questions about the organization's aspirations, goals, concerns, and challenges in an attempt to understand what they need. When we understand the need, we can then connect them to the appropriate resource. That resource may be a database, but it may also be another organization that we have connected with. Over time, as we build our "community collection," this will hap- pen more frequently.

When doing community reference, we are also doing collection development. We are curating the organization as a potential resource in the community. We listen and ask questions to both understand their needs, and understand their value as a resource in the community collection.

The real power is when you put these together. As you are listening to an orga- nization, you may find that linking them not to a library resource, but another community member or organization might be the best answer.[3]

Peter's explanation helped the librarians understand that community reference *is* "library work"; he made them feel more comfortable and confident about performing the service. To incentivize all his library branches to join in, Peter put up a simple online form. Librarians who attended events in the community would document whom they spoke with and what they learned about the organization and the community in general. Before they responded, however, they could see how many community events were added by the other library branches, which served as a form of positive peer pressure, working either on the librarians' internal motivation to do more or on their external motivation not to be seen as the library branch that did least.

Community Reference Takeaways

What Peter's story shows us is that many librarians are uncomfortable with the proactive librarianship being presented here. They feel their skills of reference and collection development have a place inside a library, but they worry that, outside that setting, they will be unequipped for success. In reality, however, traditional librarian skills have a bright future in community reference and in the idea that the community is the collection. Only, just as traditional librarian skills must be disconnected from any one institutional type to thrive, so, too, the librarian skills of information organization, reference, and instruction must be understood and applied outside a library-owned collection if they're to be put to best use.

Say you're a librarian who has worked at the reference desk for thirty years. Your core librarian skills are still valuable, but you won't truly know their value until you use them in the larger context of your community. As a librarian, you can catalog not just books and other materials, but also people and projects; you can use your indexing skills not just on series and manuscripts, but also to build websites and your reference skills not just inside your library, but also on Twitter, on a bike, and in town hall. Far from being a waste or irrelevant, those thirty years have prepared you to shoot ahead: without your desk time, you wouldn't be ready for your community time.

An Assured Path to Irrelevance or an Outright Impeachment of Our Basic Principles?

I would be remiss if I didn't talk about some of the dangers facing public libraries. Of the special concerns voiced in and about public libraries, perhaps the two biggest are "What happens when public libraries are the last civic service agencies standing?" and "As public libraries expand their services to include everything from tax help to makerspaces, how are public librarians supposed to know it all?" These two concerns are related.

To save money, one after another, government agencies are closing their local offices and moving their "services" to the web. The quotation marks are there because, even though the agencies often post documents online, they rarely provide sufficient human support for citizens trying to understand or use the documents. If I have a question about filling out a form, simply having access to the form online is no help. Librarians realized this a long time ago (collections of books and other materials aren't enough to educate or inform community members—we need librarians). But the net effect of retreating governmental services is that librarians are often left holding the bag in terms of support.

In today's municipalities, the public library is left standing virtually alone as a community-wide civic organization. In many, perhaps ironic ways, the retreat of mediated social and civic services has pushed public libraries to reach out to their communities; both the mission and functions of public libraries are being expanded. This is a good thing—public libraries have the opportunity to become more central in the lives of their community members. But an expansion of services without a corresponding expansion of resources (budget, personnel, authority, training) is a recipe for disaster.

The doomsday vision for tomorrow's public libraries is not obsolescence, but overexpansion: doing far too many things far too poorly. Rather than serving as advocates to shore up and strengthen the democratic process, public libraries can become the latest targets of a citizenry looking for examples of failure in government. The question then becomes not why do we have public libraries, but why are our tax dollars supporting their substandard services?

The apocalyptic vision for tomorrow's public libraries is not obsolescence, but rather an overexpanded shell doing a million things poorly. Like a balloon, libraries expand in mandates without support, creating an ever-thinning membrane and an empty core. Rather than working to shore up the democratic process, libraries become the latest target of a citizenry looking for examples of failure in government. The question shall become not why we have libraries, but why tax dollars support substandard service.

So how do public librarians avoid this terminal overexpansion? Some call for retrenchment. Get back to core literacy (reading), refocus on collections, and promote the role of libraries as safe havens from the world of crime and drugs. This is an equally bad idea, doomed to failure. Rather than inviting complaints of too little service in too many areas, public libraries will get dismissed as too narrow to be of any real use to their communities. No, our public libraries need a plan to take hold of this opportunity and grow to meet the needs of our communities.

This plan requires two major efforts. The first is obvious and many have started down this road: advocacy for more resources. We must mobilize citizens and government to support and fund our public libraries as the public face of our communities—a marketplace of ideas and services, where private and public come together seamlessly.

But if all public libraries do is appoint themselves the next great bureaucracy, they will fail here as well. Public librarians will lose their special status as their libraries are forced to hire more and more people from social services, education, technology, and other fields. There is a very real and legitimate worry that public librarians, indeed, librarians of all stripes, are being called to do too much. Can any one professional really be librarian, programmer, maker, social worker, and employment consultant at the same time? No, we librarians can't do it all—but we can help our communities do it all. The second major effort requires us to look at every new service or program offered by a library not as a new set of skills that we must learn as librarians, but rather as an opportunity for us to empower our community members to learn those skills themselves.

That is the big change and opportunity in librarianship. Librarians must stop looking at those who walk into their buildings or those who visit via the web as consumers and users who require help from an all-knowing bookworm. For too many the answer is not in the community of librarians, but in the collections we build. But if we leave it to the collection then we are making the same mistake those government agencies are making ...

retreating to the town hall, leaving pamphlets and forms to fill the void when people want service and opportunity.

Librarians have the ability (with resources) to form teams of experts on the payroll, but more importantly by drawing on expertise within the community itself, to educate, and improve. Librarians value in this equation is a little of the tools we bring (spaces, standards, collections), and *A LOT* in the expertise we bring. Librarians can help truly define community needs and gaps. Librarians can identify experts, and work with them to provide expertise to everyone (in lectures, hands-on skills, consulting, production, new publishing efforts). All the while knitting together the community in a tight fabric of knowing ... that is the value of the librarian. Do librarians need to know everything? No! They need to know how to unlock the knowledge of the community and set it free while imbuing the entire community with the values of learning, openness, intellectual honesty, and intellectual safety.

This idea of the library being a safety net by weaving together the fabric of community expertise works in other library communities as well. Faculty need research and support, students need motivation and to be valued. Lawyers need trial support, doctors, oh God help me, doctors need the humanity of librarians working with people in crisis. Do librarians become doctors, lawyers, and faculty? Perhaps in some special cases, yes. However, more generally, we become the connective tissue that binds the community together. Librarians become engineers in the social infrastructure of greatness that could be our communities.

This is our opportunity and challenge. The potential reward is not in dollars or square feet, but in better communities and improved lives. This is a vision worth fighting for, and that others will join. Right now, today, your communities are looking around to see which institution of democratic participation, which institution of learning, which principled corps of professionals can see them through a particularly scary moment in history. For all the promise of progress seen in every new iPhone there is the crippling poverty spreading like a cancer to fill the wage inequity of the land. For every new medical miracle cure there is an Ebola shining the reality that nature is not simply controlled. For every fair and free election there is an authoritarian state showing us that freedom and participation is not in our genes, but in our constant mortal struggle to rise above our animal nature.

Our communities need us. In colleges and universities they need us to span the vaulted towers of disciplines. In schools they need us to shatter the isolating walls of the classroom to bring students and teachers into the light of inquiry. In our states and our towns they need librarians to provide safe shelter for the bodies and the minds of the frightened—we must embolden them with the armor of knowledge and the defense of their neighbors. If libraries are to be the last civic institution standing, then we shall stand tall, and together, locked arm in arm with our patrons, and students, and faculty, and principles, and congressmen, and all those who value the society we live in. We will not be so arrogant as to believe we can know it all, or that any one person, regardless of rank or title, can be alone in all the knowledge they ever need.

17 Engines of Advancement

Core Chapter Concept: Libraries must make visible the value they bring to their communities.

I'm going to end the discussion of library types and libraries overall with public libraries. But I'd like to make a few remarks here about "special libraries," a term representing perhaps the worst failure of a reductionist approach to librarianship. Just as you have academic libraries in colleges, school libraries in schools, and public libraries in towns and cities, so you have special libraries in government agencies, hospitals and medical clinics, music halls, law offices, banks, NGOs, construction and manufacturing companies, museums, sports organizations, and just about every other conceivable organized community. What sets special libraries apart from other libraries? They are all very closely aligned to specific missions of specific communities.

Thus the Smithsonian Museum of American Art has a special library within it (and, yes, it is publicly funded, but *not* considered a public library), whose librarians build systems to help artists and museum curators. Most hospitals also have medical libraries to help doctors, nurses, health care providers, and even the general public build knowledge about medicine. In "Going to the Conversation" in chapter 6, I talked about how the role of these medical libraries is moving from passive question-answering centers to active participation in medical teams.

Why not have a full chapter on special libraries, then? It's not that special libraries are less important than school, public, or academic libraries. Far from it. The real reason is that many special libraries have already made the transition to librarians-first librarianship. Embassy libraries have replaced librarians in physical locations with librarians on standby. Special librarians are leaving their library quarters to be embedded in research teams. In essence, special libraries are deep in transition to becoming community libraries because of industry pressures to locate expertise at the point of need and to closely align that expertise with industry outcomes.

As discussed before, unlike the single mission of librarians, the mission of any given library is co-constructed by its librarians and community. As a reflection of its community, that mission will vary from community to community. But there is a common reason that all librarians build libraries: community improvement. The community members of businesses, municipalities, colleges, schools, hospitals, even royal palaces have libraries because they believe libraries make them better. For them, "make them better" may mean a better bottom line, a more literate, informed citizenry, better teachers and students, improved patient outcomes, or perhaps a better understanding of their royal subjects. Whatever the case, there is great power when librarians and communities come together to form platforms of improvement and innovation. But this great power is not always visible. Worse still, the key components of this engine of community advancement are often taken for granted.

A closed library may present the enticing possibility of learning with its impressive architecture and many shelves of books. Yet closed, the library is dead, a warehouse. To make it live takes not only community members using and supporting the library, but librarians crafting that support into services, and structures, and action. It is only when individuals of good intent come together in principled interactions that libraries, their librarians, and their community members can truly use knowledge to ignite possibilities.

By continually attaching what librarians and their communities do to abstract institutions or, worse still, to buildings called "libraries," we devalue the participants in those systems, and we ignore the real and hard choices that all of them must make to define what community improvement is. For too long have librarians hidden behind the stacks and a false flag of neutrality. For too long have communities been passive "consumers" of libraries, all but totally unaware of the effort it takes to *make* a community better. For too long have librarians seen communities as receivers of information and not creators of knowledge. And for too long have communities seen their librarians as little more than clerks and readers.

It's time to redefine what libraries are and to retask them with helping their communities through learning and knowledge creation. It's time to expect more of these institutions, and those who gather and work within their places. It's time to free librarians from the shackles of hidebound tradition and to send them out into their communities to listen, learn, and act. And it's well past time we librarians expected more from our community members than a vote on a budget and passing admiration. Our communities are full of talent and expertise and aspirations, waiting to serve a world desperately in need of all three.

18   Coda

In February 2014, in an attempt to clear my body of the cancer that was devouring my immune system and transforming my lymph nodes into tumors that could crush my heart or lungs, I was given Melphalan—a derivative of mustard gas used in the trench warfare of World War I—in so powerful a dose it would kill the very marrow in my bones. Nurses fed me ice chips to minimize the blistering of my mouth from the drug's toxicity.

The next day, I had my own stem cells injected into my heart to find their way back to the core of my bones. There they began regrowing the marrow, which then slowly produced new blood cells. It was my new birthday.

Over the next days and then weeks, my new marrow also made white blood cells to start repairing the organs scarred by the toxicity of Melphalan and the other chemo poisons targeting my cancer. Then the life-saving transfusions given me by anonymous donors from around the country were replaced by my own red blood cells. And, finally, new platelets sealed my leaking blood vessels, shrinking the blisters on my gums and feet.

Over the first year of this new life, I got stronger, I got healthier. My hair returned, at least to what I had before the cancer. I learned to climb the stairs without the help of my sons. Eventually, I could eat food not prepared at home—provided it was cooked hot enough to kill any pathogens that could overwhelm my recovering immune system. I was able to walk again, first in my home, then in my neighborhood. And, at last, but with great trepidation, I was able to go back to work.

I was to give the first keynote speech of my new life at a meeting of the New York Section of School Librarians. The convention center was a fifteen-minute drive from my home. The topic was up to me. But my mind was filled with questions.

What could I say? Did I have anything new to say? Why say anything at all? Why not just retreat into my ivory tower, teach my classes, serve on my committees, and never have to get on another plane again? What did I have to say to school librarians? Did I even care anymore?

I called up an old friend and colleague and shared my crisis of faith. He told me he had already moved on from librarians. I watched online as librarians ravaged the field's "rock stars" and each other on Twitter. Why expose myself again to those who doubted, those who had lost faith, those who simply enjoyed a fight, any fight. Why not be done with it?

Then I remembered that morning, that morning of my new birthday. I remembered the doctor as he slowly pressed the syringe with my stem cells—my life—into my heart. I remembered the nurses who cleared the hallway and made sure all those attending me had masks and sanitized their hands. I remembered the priest who slipped in halfway through the procedure to put oil on my forehead. I remembered my mother there watching, my brother-in-law telling jokes to lift my spirits. I remembered my wife holding my hand, her concerned face only partly hidden behind a surgical mask.

All of these people were there to save my life. Some were there because it was their job, but all of them were there because they cared. They knew they could make a difference, and they had within them faith and hope. That doctor and those nurses saw people waste away and die from cancer every day, yet still they hoped to save everyone they could. My mother, who had lost her husband, was there because she believed her son could still live. My wife was there because she believed that we had too many years ahead of us to give up now.

Here I was months later, preparing a speech for librarians and questioning whether it was worth my time, when I was alive only because those doctors, nurses, and hundreds of librarians believed that I and other cancer patients like me were worth their time. And I knew why I cared about librarians. I cared because they had faith and hope and because every day they worked to make their communities better. In medical schools, in hospitals elsewhere, and in the hospital of my new birth were librarians who helped prepare that doctor and those nurses to save my life, who helped make it possible to turn deadly mustard gas into hope for the living.

All around me in this field, I find more people who care than people who don't. Every day, I see librarians ignoring the sarcasm and doubt and the apathy of their peers to make the world a better place for students, and faculty, and parents, and children, and cancer patients.

Since my new birthday, I've talked to hundreds of librarians eager to make a difference. I've seen whole generations of librarians in countries around the world throw off the preconceived limitations of librarianship and dedicate themselves to making a difference in their communities. I've seen hope.

This is our inheritance as librarians. Our profession is one that believes it can empower communities to make better decisions and to make the world a better place. We have stood among revolutionaries and in the halls of power. Over the millennia, we have helped bring entire civilizations out of darkness; we have helped preserve genius in the face of intolerance, and we have braved great perils to live up to our values of service and openness.

Today, more than ever, our communities need librarians dedicated to helping them achieve their aspirations and a better tomorrow. And I am here to ask you to keep the faith and to have hope. When the powerful are blind to injustice, we must be there to shine a light. When the majority oppresses and kills the minority, we must do more than document or mourn, we must act and teach. Librarians stand shoulder to shoulder with outcasts and privileged alike to seek common ground for success and equity. To those without hope, those in turmoil, and those who have lost faith or direction, we bring knowledge and power. In our libraries, our schools, our government, our hospitals, our courthouses, and even on our streets, librarians are there. Librarians choose to be there.

Choose to be there.

David Lankes
Syracuse, New York
May 25, 2015

Excursus: From Mission to Missionary

In February 2015, some fifty librarians gathered at the ALA Mid-Winter Conference to talk about this very book. What should the follow-up to *The Atlas of New Librarianship* be? How could this book help librarians trying to bring about a change in the field?

The librarians wanted a volume that was more linear, a text that quickly got across the core of librarianship focused on community and participatory. They wanted more practical examples and tools to convince other librarians, community members, and even professionals in other fields of the value of the approach. It's my hope that this guide gives them just what they wanted.

You now have the fundamentals of librarianship defined outside the context of a single institution and based on a unifying mission, learning, and values. And you have ample background to join the debate on how this proactive librarianship seeks to shape libraries and systems in general.

If you want to pursue these ideas further, I suggest you read *The Atlas of New Librarianship* and join us online to continue to explore, refine, and evolve these ideas. But if you're interested in how to take these ideas to the next level and in how to help spread them, it's time to move from me convincing you to you convincing others. That's what these excursus are for (yes, "excursus" is both singular and plural, like "fish").

The *Oxford English Dictionary* defines "excursus" as "a detailed discussion (usually in the form of an appendix at the end of a book ...) of some point which it is desired to treat more fully than can be done in a note." Why not simply call them "appendices"? Well, for one thing, it wouldn't be nearly as much fun, but the real reasons are they're meant to aid you in promoting a proactive librarianship and so are more important than the background material normally found in appendices, but they're also here for quick reference, at the end of the guide, so as not to interrupt the linear flow of its first two parts.

The first excursus, "Facilitating New Librarianship Learning," is a set of practical tips, derived from large-scale training projects, for those involved in designing curricula to promote a new view of librarianship among our colleagues. The second, "Observations from the Field," provides teaching notes for those who are using this volume as a textbook in a classroom or in continuing education. And the last excursus, "FAQs (Frequently Argued Questions)," offers ready responses to typical questions I've been asked about New Librarianship.

These curriculum ideas, field notes, and FAQs are tools you can use to promote and implement a librarianship that seeks to actively and positively transform our communities as they pursue their dreams and aspirations. But these tools are only a starting point. We live in an era where no book is ever truly finished, and no discussion ever truly closed, where we can directly engage online and continue the millennia-long conversation about librarianship and how librarians can improve society. If you need a place to start:

http://www.NewLibrarianship.org

Facilitating New Librarianship Learning

Librarianship is proactive transformative social engagement. Librarians make communities better in partnership with their community members. In preparing other librarians to engage their communities, you must be proactive as well. It takes far more than reading a book (or any number of books) to overcome nearly a century of librarians' preoccupation with efficiency (often at the expense of effectiveness), collections (defined as materials not people), institutions (libraries over librarians), and neutrality (or at least the illusion of it). As a librarian, you must take an active role in shaping your own community and in preparing this generation of librarians and the next to engage their communities—and the world.

What follows are means for the continuous training and development of librarians developed through four significant efforts to date. The first such effort, the Salzburg Curriculum, has already been discussed in some detail in chapter 8. The second effort combined keynote speeches and workshops in the form of an Expect More World Tour. The third, ILEAD USA, has so far involved ten states and nearly 769 librarians. And the fourth, the New Librarianship Master Class, was offered online to nearly 3,000 people from across the globe. All four of these efforts have provided consistent means of success in moving librarians from a focus on collections to a focus on communities.

Key Means of Success

The following nine means have been particularly effective working with in-the-field librarians:

- Emphasize teachable skills
- Link to long-standing concepts

- Build cohorts
- Use projects and inquiry when possible
- Cross boundaries
- Demonstrate comfort with ambiguity
- Build communities, not websites
- Address perceived barriers
- Provide opportunities for introspection and inspiration

These nine means build on what librarians know about good instruction generally and how people learn through conversation. With that in mind, staff development should be targeted, interactive, and build on the learners' current understandings. Let's consider each of these approaches in greater depth, providing examples where necessary.

Emphasize Teachable Skills

When you talk about incorporating communities into every facet of librarianship, too many librarians will try to compartmentalize working with community members as the job of the "community engagement librarian," as though it was only another of the many different facets of librarianship. This is not the case. Everything librarians do must take their communities into account. From arranging materials, to furnishing rooms, to coding software, all tasks should be guided with input from and awareness of community members.

I recall a student in my introductory course telling me, "You know, I was ready to quit and say this field is not for me. I'm not looking to work with people directly. Then I started looking at the other courses I'd be taking, like cataloging, and I saw my place in the field ... behind the scenes working on the collection." She looked relieved. I felt bad breaking the news that everything librarians should be doing involves working with their community members.

I told her about a conversation a new dean of a library school had with local technical service librarians. When the dean asked them how the school's curriculum could be improved, they replied that, though the school was doing a good job teaching the part of cataloging from resources to descriptive metadata (which at the time meant using MARC, AACR2, and so on), it was failing to teach the most important part of cataloging—from resources to community members. Where documents fit in classification schemes, the subject terms used to describe resources, keywords, and so on all depended on knowing how community members were talking about and looking for these resources. As my colleague Barbara Kwasnik is fond of saying, a catalog record is really just a pre-reference interview. The goal is to anticipate how community members will look or ask for resources. In other words, catalogers, like reference librarians, have to know and work with community members in a meaningful, personal way.

This means that *all* librarians need skills in community engagement, communication, and identifying community needs and aspirations. Although the so-called soft skills of facilitating and interacting with individuals and groups are hard to nail down and often needed across many domains, they can be taught, and learning them is more a matter of practice than cultivating some innate predisposition. The key for learners is to know why they are working with their community members. The key for you as teacher is demonstrating methods of eliciting input from members that go far beyond the ability to engage in small talk.

Cheryl Gould is not only an outstanding facilitator of meetings and conversations; she is also a student of facilitation in general. A key to her approach is improvisation, which Cheryl shows is something that can be both taught and learned. In her contribution, she talks about how she applied improvisation directly to engaging librarians on the mission of librarians as part of the Expect More World Tour.

Shrinking the Room
by Cheryl Gould

Most of us have been to presentations or trainings where all we do is sit and listen. If we have a fabulous speaker, this can be pleasant and even inspiring if we care deeply about the topic. In most cases, we're just happy to have "a day away from the office," but little learning or behavior change takes place. Learning takes place when people are invited into and engaged with a topic, when they have a chance to investigate ideas in a safe space where all ideas are respected and all opinions valued. A good facilitator with a good design can create this safe space for people to try out new behaviors and ideas.

You start by doing something different that "shrinks the room," makes people slightly nervous, but that also guarantees success. I usually choose an activity that gets people up out of their seats and talking to someone they don't know. I'll ask them to share something simple for a minute. I often have this initial activity relate to the topic of the event, but it could just as easily be about a book they're reading, where they'd like to go on a vacation, or a recent work success (or failure, depending on your topic). This works best when you ask people to talk to someone they don't know.

I start every event with an activity like this within the first five minutes or so. It lets people know they'll be expected to participate. In the Expect More World Tour workshops, we start by asking people to get in groups of three and spend two minutes talking about what "engagement" means. We then have a short debrief and talk about how we will, in the space of the next few hours, engage with one another to facilitate knowledge creation for the community of learners in the room. In this way, the activity directly relates to the topic of the day, which is to discuss the various parts of the mission of librarians. Doing this activity gets people not only thinking about engagement but also feeling engaged, and it models the kinds of engagement we want librarians to use in their communities. In the Expect More events, we are modeling community engagement at its best; this includes

- conversations about complicated challenges for which there are no single solutions;

- posing thought-provoking questions;

- unearthing mental models of knowledge and of community that might keep people constrained;

- discussing first challenges and then solutions based on the knowledge and experience of the community in the room;

- facilitating that makes it clear that everyone is expected to participate and that all voices will be heard and respected, and that it's okay to have a little fun along the way.

Instead of telling, we spend more time asking and facilitating conversation. If your goal is to teach someone to catalog or to use a computer, you'll end up doing a lot of telling because there's is a right way and a wrong way and endless details to learn. In New Librarianship, when we talk about engaging with the community, you'll be in discussions where there may be no right or wrong answers. The skills required to engage in those conversations are to have a facilitator's toolkit for mediating the process and a killer set of communication skills to help people feel heard and not judged, to listen appreciatively even when you disagree, to not shy away from differences of opinion, and to have a truly facilitative mindset where you believe that your role is to make it easy for people to be successful, however they define success.

My belief is that only by pairing a facilitative mindset with excellent communication and facilitation skills can we make New Librarianship a reality and fulfill our mission as librarians.

Link to Long-Standing Concepts

In chapter 16, you saw how Peter Bromberg was able to move community reference forward by showing that, even though the venue (community organizations) was different, the skills the librarians brought to bear (reference and collection development) were long standing and well understood. This points to one of my frustrations with the name "New Librarianship" given to this community approach. There are both supporters and detractors who seek to portray the approach as a nearly complete break from current and past practices.

To be sure, the community approach entails major shifts in the understanding of librarianship (most notably, focusing on librarians over libraries and on communities over collections). But far from asking librarians to abandon their traditional skills, librarianship asks them instead to reapply and adapt those skills to new environments.

Take the slogan "The community is the collection." Clearly, this is about librarians paying greater attention to and using the expertise resident in the communities they serve rather than focusing on accumulating resources alone. The slogan didn't just pop out of the air; it arose in response to librarians asking questions like "How can I know whether a community member's expertise is real?" or "What if the member doesn't have the skills needed to present it in public?" or "How do I find the expertise in my community to begin with?" Consider the same questions focused on collections of materials and artifacts: "How can I know if this book is credible?" "What if this resource doesn't have a usable interface for our members?" "How do I find credible resources on this topic?" The answer to both sets of questions is: collection development. Liberians have always developed skills in selection, acquisition, and organization. It has been around books, but also around scrolls, tablets, manuscripts, ephemera, and now people.

I hear all the time, even from the most traditional of librarians, how the age of Google and the Internet has made librarians more necessary than ever before, how librarians are the best search engines or the best judges of the quality of information. I would argue that these applications of librarianship in an Internet world are incremental, and frankly short-term at best. Librarians aren't good search engines. Search engines sort through billions of possible resources and match it to a query in milliseconds returning results often highly influenced by advertising and dependent on the erosion of community member privacy. As for librarians as arbiters of quality, they can only do this by a strong knowledge of what a community member already believes and will find acceptable.

The future of librarianship lies not in making librarians cogs in our consumption-oriented society, but in librarians' power as professionals to facilitate and unleash the creative abilities of our community members. And the future of libraries lies in embedding our librarian values in community institutions like businesses, governments, schools, colleges, and universities, and civic welfare groups. Let Google build good tools for our larger mission. Let Amazon build collections for commerce, while librarians ensure that every community member, whether citizen, government official, student, teacher, preacher, or homeless person, has access to the rich history and current conversations of our communities. We've been doing this in one form or another for millennia; we need to ensure that we continue to far into the future by adapting to current realities.

Build Cohorts

I used to do a fair bit of work with primary and secondary school teachers. The hard reality I found was that many teachers are isolated in their classrooms. Librarians can also become very isolated, especially in large libraries, where the isolation comes from working on a desk or in a compartmentalized library function.

By bringing librarians together, you help them build a cohort, a practice community that allows them to share ideas and conversations with likeminded peers. This is, of course, not a new concept. In academia, we've talked for generations about "invisible colleges," where scholars find peers across institutional boundaries. Many librarians need the support of likeminded agents for change, and good continuing education makes this possible by helping librarians build cohorts. But cohort building needs to go beyond continuing education. In a recent trip to Italy, I met with amazing librarians like Stella Rasetti, director of the San Giorgio Library in Pistoia, and Anna Maria Tammaro a professor at the University of Parma. I met with librarians from academic libraries, companies, and all sorts of other institutions. They all expressed a level of frustration with the status of librarians in Italy and a strong desire to engage their communities.

Working for change, however, was an increasingly tight knit group of what Stella referred to as "guerrilla librarians," a cohort that spanned the country and beyond and whose members talked with one another constantly. They sought out leadership positions in library associations. They wrote books and translated materials to support their work and their approach. Any attempt to prepare librarians for this new librarianship must help librarians build a cohort—a band of brothers and sisters across departments, institutions, and library types. Help your librarians build cohorts wherever you can.

Use Projects and Inquiry When Possible

From posters to websites, to whole new systems, librarians who facilitate the ideas and questions their community members care about by helping them put these ideas and questions into practice as projects achieve the best results. If your learners feel they can make something they love better, they'll learn more about it. This makes sense, of course, because it demonstrates everything we know about learning.

Cross Boundaries

The point of continuing education for librarians is to help them break habits that are not serving them well, to help them reexamine how and why they do things. This can be difficult. Not just difficult because you're asking your librarians to embrace change, but because you're asking them to set aside an entrenched worldview whose assumptions about library tasks and about librarianship in general have brought them some success. Often these assumptions have not been consciously developed, but have been implicitly learned over years of practice.

To be successful in convincing librarians who have "manned the desk for thirty years," or "cataloged all my life" to adopt a more proactive community approach to librarianship, you must begin by challenging these implicit assumptions. The fastest way to do this is to have them work with librarians from other environments. Academic librarians quickly find that, despite their differences, they have a lot in common with public librarians, as do school librarians with law librarians, and so on. But interacting with librarians from different environments also forces learners to make their implicit assumptions explicit, which gives you, as a facilitator, an opportunity to challenge them or link them to new practices.

Demonstrate Comfort with Ambiguity

When I was junior in college, I took a C programming language course. On the first day of class, the teacher drew a simple illustration on the chalkboard.

"Who can tell me what this is?" he asked us.

As we gave our guesses, the teacher slowly made his way toward the back of the classroom.

"A keyboard," someone offered.

"Right, and what's that key on the far right?" he asked, still moving toward the back of the room.

"Escape key?" "Alt key?" the guesses rang out.

"No," he said as he made it to the back wall. "That's the key that blows the whole damn computer up!" he shouted, hurling his chalk at the board, where it promptly shattered.

Now, with the class's full attention, the teacher returned calmly to the front of the class while saying, "Of course, there is no such key, but many of us work like there *is*." He went on to talk about how we were going to make a lot of mistakes, "blow up" a lot of programs, but that was how we learned. Moreover, the systems we would be working on were built for this kind of thing, and we shouldn't worry about "killing" our computers.

In these days of white boards, I haven't quite found the courage to try to shatter a marker with my library science students, but, in every other way, I let them know that our class is a safe place to try out ideas and thoughts and criticisms, and they shouldn't worry about "blowing up" the classroom. In giving them what they need to succeed in the class (feedback on assignments, rubrics, clear instructions), I tell them there'll be a lot of ambiguity, but that they should see that ambiguity as a space for innovation and for trial and error.

In our libraries and in our learning, we must stop seeing ambiguity as disorder as something to be minimized if not completely avoided. We need a solid foundation and a safe harbor, but we also need to embrace the ambiguous—the unclear and unformed—as an invitation to experiment, to push our knowledge further.

Many people will say that failure should be celebrated, not feared, as a natural consequence of learning and a way of pushing ourselves to go further than we've gone before. Failure should indeed be welcomed, but only if there is some solid ground to come back to or a clear means of learning from it. Because, ultimately, none of us celebrates failure; we celebrate the courage to try new things and reach beyond our current grasp.

Build Communities, Not Websites

Most librarians who look to community engagement almost always end up thinking about the web and using the Internet to reach their communities. This in itself is not a bad idea, but in my experience, they often take a collection-oriented, one-way access mentality with them.

"We can use Facebook to connect to the community!"

"Great, how?"

"We'll put organizational announcements on our wall."

Sigh.

"We'll use this content management system to allow kids to sign up for our gaming programs and talk about gaming!"

"Where do the kids talk about gaming now?"

"Mostly online in the games or with their friends at school."

"So, why would they want to move that conversation to your system? What does your system provide that they don't already have?"

Blank stares

Let me be very clear. You need to tell your librarians that they can marshal all the ideas of usability, user experience, accessibility, responsive design, good graphic design, and laser light shows they like in building their new websites, but these websites will fail if they're not meeting their members' needs, or if they're not at the point of their conversations. Here's the test. Ask them to put in the word "participant" every place they want to write or say "user" or "patron" and to change the word "use" into "create." If the result doesn't make any sense, they're doing it wrong.

Address Perceived Barriers

One of the activities Cheryl Gould introduced in the Expect More World Tour workshops was having participants identify perceived barriers to implementing the ideas presented in this book. This table summarizes the feedback she received across all five sessions:

Barrier	Percentage
Lack of staff	20.69
Fear of failure	17.24
Lack of time	12.07
Loss of control	6.90
Selling it to others	6.90
Lack of vision	6.90
Keeping up with technology	6.90
Fear of community	5.17
Lack of planning	3.45
Whom to talk to	3.45
Community expectations	3.45
Lack of flexible schedule	1.72
Fear of overcommitment	1.72
Setting boundaries	1.72
Lack of funding	1.72

The percentages in the table are based on a small sample size and are presented here just to give you a sense of the distribution of perceived barriers. The topics identified by workshop participants are consistent with issues raised online and in other World Tour activities. Before moving on to the other projects and other generalizable means of training, it's worth addressing the top identified barriers.

Lack of Staff   I've heard many librarians say that the expanded community engagement called for in this approach to librarianship requires additional staff and time. With librarians focused on the daily tasks of running libraries and library systems (reference, cataloging, shelving, and so on), who's available to go into the community? Given the financial situation of most libraries, creating positions for community engagement or community reference simply isn't possible, they say, especially in one-librarian or other small libraries.

The belief that community engagement requires additional staff is a fundamental misunderstanding of the role of librarians. Community engagement is not simply another of librarians' many functions; rather, it lies at the core of *all* librarian functions. Just as Sue Kowalski in her school library enlisted the help of her student iStaff volunteers on library main-tenance tasks so that she could better focus on engagement with teachers and delivering curriculum, librarians in all settings need to take a serious look at the time they spend on tool and system maintenance, enlisting help from their community members as needed in order to devote more time and energy to engagement. Often knowing their members far better than librarians in larger libraries do theirs, the librarians in small libraries are also often in a better position to engage their members.

Community engagement is not a job for a special kind of librarian; it is the job of all librarians in all of their functions. No librarian can be all things to all people; that's why librarians must turn to their community members to help provide and extend services. Librarians need to give up on the idea that they must know everything or master every topic before they share it with their members. Does this mean there are things that a library currently does that will need to be scaled back? Yes. Can I name those things? No. Why? Because every library will have to make that deter-mination with its community members. In some communities, collection activities or virtual services through the Internet will need to be scaled back, in others not. The days that one size fits all libraries are over. Librar-ians and their professional identities now form the common core of the field, and the systems they build, including the libraries they maintain, will be as varied as the communities they serve. But by focusing on facilitation, librarians become amplifiers—expanding their impact through the com-munity members they empower.

Fear of Failure Shifting the focus of librarianship to librarians can be exciting, but also very scary. Many librarians have enjoyed the stability that comes from defining their jobs by tasks such as cataloging, reference, story time, and bibliographic instruction. Tasks can be shared and made routine; policies can be attached to them that minimize choice and conflict. Indeed, many librarians look at policies as a risk avoidance strategy. If a book is challenged at the circulation desk, they don't have to engage the challenger in debate or discussion, they can shift the conversation to a premade policy. Don't get me wrong, policies have their place, but they should be ways of documenting decisions and conversations between librarians and commu-nity members, not means of avoiding debate. Overreliance on tasks and preemptive policies reflects a fear of failure.

Change can be discomforting, particularly change that's seen as episodic and even arbitrary. Change is also discomforting when librarians fear that a failed project will result in their being punished or losing the confidence of their community members.

The way to allay fear of failure is to implement procedures and reward systems for experimentation, to encourage librarians both to try constantly to improve current systems and to try new things. When you make clear to community members and staff alike what the core values of your library are and how current services should be judged against those values, then you create room for accepting that experiments that may fail. Adding a 3-D printer to your library can be seen either as an experiment to enrich the learning mission of your library or as a fad. The difference in perception is all about expectations and connection to your community.

Provide Opportunities for Introspection and Inspiration

I can give a killer keynote speech. I've gotten pretty good of "putting on my Baptist preacher" and rallying librarians. I use humor at the right spots, I talk about a positive future for our profession, and I call out the pride we librarians have within ourselves. I can, on good days, inspire.

We all need to hear inspirational speeches and motivational messages from time to time. A good keynote speech that conveys the passion and potential for the field is a great thing. But it's only half of the equation. Good continuing education should inspire, but it should also provoke introspection. Having learners ask themselves why the talk was inspiring, how they should respond, and how they can kindle that kind of passion in their community members is equally important.

What you're asking your librarians to do in adopting this approach to librarianship is a tall order. You're asking them to leave the safety of stacks and policies and long-standing practices and to go out into their communities—to listen to their community members and ask them for their participation. You're asking librarians to stand up and say that the value they bring to their communities is not to be found within the walls of their library buildings, nor in deep databases, nor in catalogs, but only in the librarians themselves. You're asking librarians to set aside their long-held belief in neutrality and impartiality and to actively pledge themselves to a very local definition of community improvement. No speeches can prepare them for that.

It's only by looking at librarians as people that we can prepare them to succeed in improving society. Any adoption of this new librarianship must be accompanied by a recommitment to values too often taught in the abstract. We must say that we personally will make a difference, and we must say it not out of arrogance or self-importance, but in recognition that to help our communities achieve their very human aspirations and solve their very human problems, we must first identify our own aspirations and problems.

Beck Tench understands this. With a background in innovation and museums. Beck has for the past several years been part of the ILEAD USA project to strengthen librarians' understanding of leadership and technology. The project challenges librarians to work on real projects in teams across a range of organizations and constantly shows them a new way to look at our profession. The experience can be unnerving for many participants. But Beck is there, as she says, to "pick up the pieces."

Team Time with Beck
by Beck Tench

Every year at ILEAD USA, I give a talk about fear, failure, and change. For the last few years, I've followed that talk up with something called "Team Time with Beck."

Team Time with each ILEAD USA team runs just over an hour and is the result of previous ILEADERs requesting "more time with Beck" in the feedback cards passed out each day of the yearly project. Being Beck, I didn't know why teams wanted more time with me, and I don't think they did either, but, in true ILEAD USA fashion, we made a space for it and watched what happened.

At first, I treated the time like a Q&A, but the teams didn't have questions for me. After a little flailing about and a lot of improvising, I figured out what they wanted: they wanted to talk, and they wanted to be heard.

"How Do You Feel?"

I start the groups by asking them how they're feeling about their projects. I truly listen to what each of them says. I reflect back what I hear and when I don't understand something, I ask questions. I work hard to stop myself from interrupting them, from suggesting solutions or my own ideas. I keep listening, try to understand how they're feeling, and nudge them into a space of uncertainty when they seem to be too comfortable or, for the most fearful ones, even when they seem to have tuned out altogether.

"What Are You Afraid Of?"

I'm most interested in having these librarians try things that might not work. I know through my own experiences of failure and also a long history with ILEAD USA leadership that, even when they fail, they are truly safe. I want them to experience librarianship without the scaffolding of certainty and predictability their typical work provides. I want them to go out on a limb in their time at ILEAD USA. So, I ask them to tell me what they're afraid of and I push them to go places that cause them worry and fear.

Nervous, but Excited

Sometimes they can go too far with the worry, and their fear feels too big. Sometimes they don't go far enough and it feels too small. I try to size up where they are as individuals and where they are as a group. I know that they have limited resources in both time and money. I also know that, since they are librarians, it is likely they want to save the world and appear to be effortlessly perfect while doing so. Through conversation, we balance these pieces so that they let go a little of their expectations and perfectionism, but hold on to enough of both that they're working toward something that matters. The emotional state that seems to resonate with most everyone is "nervous, but excited." When they're there, individually and as a team, they're where they need to be.

Not Group Therapy, but We Do Have Kleenex Handy

Mr. Rogers once said, "You rarely have time for everything you want in life, so you have to make choices. Hopefully, those choices can come from a deep sense of who you are."[1]

I'm not a librarian, but I've sat with, listened to, and paid a lot of attention to hundreds of them. I've observed that even though they entered this profession for a multitude of reasons, they are all different persons now than when they chose to become librarians. They bring the persons and librarians they are now into Team Time with Beck. I consider it my job to understand who they are today, and to support each of them in choices that honor that.

Observations from the Field

What follows are field notes, tricks, and observations I've made while trying to convey the ideas of a librarianship built around librarians and our communities. Although I've incorporated much of this in the text of the chapters themselves, there are some points that merit further discussion.

Chapter 2

Most librarians will assume they already have a clear definition of "library" and "librarianship," but when you test them, they'll begin to see that their definitions are fuzzy. Most will define "library" as a place to acquire, organize, and disseminate information, knowledge, or resources. But when you ask them to parse the various parts of their definition, the gaps will begin to show. What is information? What is knowledge? Is place important? Can you have a library without a physical space?

Once your learner librarians begin to explore their beliefs, however, they'll become much more open to a message that provides some certainty. This is normally a good place to start introducing them to new concepts of librarianship.

Chapter 3

One of the most common reactions/misunderstandings I encounter with the mission presented in chapter 1 is that I am pushing it as a field-wide mission for libraries *and* library institutions. I'm not. The mission is for *librarians*, not the places they work in; the missions of libraries should vary from institution to institution, just as the communities that libraries serve do.

That said, the mission of librarians and the missions of the places they work in (whether libraries, educational or other institutions, or firms) should not be completely disconnected. Your librarians should seek to shape the larger institutional missions. In this way, they can bring their values and beliefs to libraries and other institutions or organizations as they seek to improve society and the position of librarians within society.

Chapter 4

The discussion of knowledge is a tricky one to have with your librarians. Many will simply feel they don't need to know much about knowledge, at least not anything in great detail. They're fine in the information world and will often avoid any discussion of knowledge to focus on things like service. They believe that if members learn as a result of their work, that's fine, but not their business. I see this often in reference librarians who believe their role is to get community members the materials they've requested and let the members work things out for themselves. The problem is not that members won't "work things out for themselves," they probably will, but rather that they'll miss the value that librarians can bring them in the process.

The other tricky part of talking about knowledge is discussing it with those of your librarians who *do* care. Many will take exception to the constructivist approach to knowledge given in this guide. This exception will often turn into an argument about truth and epistemology. My position is not that they're right or wrong, but that such philosophical arguments about the nature of our understanding of the universe aren't helpful in dealing with the complexity of librarians' day-to-day work. My approach takes what amounts to a pragmatic approach to knowledge. I contend that librarians work in the complex space of meaning above fact, and that if we are to educate our community members—help them learn—we need to accept that there are many beliefs, no one of them right or wrong in itself.

Chapter 5

Librarians from primarily technical and public service backgrounds get the general idea of facilitation quickly. However, it is hard for many to get past access, and particularly one-way access. Much of the current field of librarianship is focused on access to materials and collections. We have policies on equitable access; we have whole courses devoted to classification and the arrangement of resources. But most of these are about ensuring that members have access to existing resources to be used by them.

The real trick is getting your learner librarians to think about when members have something they wish to share. How do the librarians then provide access to those members? And how can they do this and still be protective of their members' privacy?

If you can get your librarians thinking of access as a two-way process, then engaging them in thinking about knowledge creation through direct instruction and about environment is relatively easy. For, of course, at least some of their members will need help in accessing resources or in using technology, and, of course, almost all of them will also need to feel safe.

The next major obstacle is motivation. Many if not most of your librarians will assume the members they interact with are already motivated, that these members want to know something either for themselves (internal motivation) or because someone is asking them to know it (a teacher giving an assignment—external motivation). It's important that your librarians know which kind of motivation it is and how strong. But it's just as important for them to know how to stimulate motivation—to motivate their members to learn.

Chapter 6

There are whole books devoted to system design, although most are centered on technical systems like websites and apps. One method I've used with some success in getting librarians to think about designing participatory systems of all types is "conversation mapping."[1] The idea is that, rather than starting with an idea for a system on their own, the librarians base it on what their community members are talking about (and are therefore seeking to create knowledge about).

Have your librarians begin by identifying first the communities they're serving and then the subcommunities of those communities. For example, a community might be a high school; its subcommunities might be freshmen, science teachers, and parents. Next, have them identify what conversations each of these subcommunities is having, for example, the school budget, the Common Core, and testing. And, finally, have them rank each of these conversations on a 1 to 3 scale, first, as to how important the conversation is for that subcommunity and, second, as to how well it is served by the librarians.

Once they have their conversation maps, your librarians can go back and identify the conversations with high importance to their communities and low support by the librarians (the 3s and 1s). This is the beginning of other conversations they can have with their members, conversations about how they, as librarians, can be seen as important in conversations their communities find important—and also the beginning of conversations about what systems and services they can offer within their communities.

Chapter 7

Your librarians will rightly see themselves as principled professionals, but they'll often see those principles in binary terms: "Either I support privacy or I don't"; "Either I support universal access or I don't." Yet when our principles are put into action on the line, a gray continuum between black and white appears for each principle. Are filters always bad? Do library services always have to be about learning?

You can see where these binary views can get in the way of providing services. For example, many of your librarians will see their members' adoption of social media as a sign of ignorance about privacy, that their members don't realize they're actually giving away their right to privacy by using social media services like Facebook. Yet study after study shows that people using such services are making conscious, rational choices, that they see privacy not as an absolute good but as something to be traded off, at least in part, for another good, free access to a social network. Have your librarians ask themselves, can their library services benefit from this more nuanced view? Can keeping reading records of their members help them give those members better recommendations for other materials?

What also becomes clear from the field implementations of this approach to librarianship is that librarians often feel that they are being of service as long as they serve well the community members they regularly interact with. In a public library, this would be the members who actually come into the library. But you need to tell your librarians just how few of their members this might turn out to be. If they have really good library card outreach programs, for example, 70 percent of the community members they serve might have cards. But, typically, only 30 percent of the members will actually use the cards, only half of those will do so regularly, and only half of *those* will regularly come in to use their libraries' facilities. So even though 100 percent of the taxpayers in their communities are supporting their libraries, the librarians might be regularly interacting with fewer than 10 percent of the members they serve. The percentages will vary from library to library, but the ones in this example represent working averages given me by many public library directors.

Chapter 8

There is a perennial dialogue about skills versus theory in the field of librarianship, often tied to a discussion of the library science programs preparing librarians for the work they'll be doing. Though a rich and important dialogue, it often overlooks the fact that there is no one answer for what all librarians should know, nor one curriculum for all programs to prepare them. Even the Salzburg Curriculum is more a set of aspirations than of true measurable competencies.

The reason this dialogue is important and will never end is that the field of librarianship is always changing to match the needs of communities (and the employment prospects for librarians). In times of relative calm, it makes sense for librarians to focus on acquiring skills and mastery of tools. On the other hand, in times of great change (technological, cultural, political), it makes sense for them to focus more on *why* things are done than on how they are done. As tools and communities change, professional and continuing education for librarians must be seen as more about outcomes than outputs.

There is another important part of this dialogue that's become increasingly apparent in a question raised by National Archivist of the United States David Ferriero—who are the real "customers" of library science programs?[2] Ferriero contended that, even though library science departments in universities may claim that the students are the customers of their programs, the real customers are the libraries, archives, and museums where the program graduates will work as librarians. Therefore, library science programs should focus on the needs of the institutions. In essence, libraries should define librarians, not the other way around.

This view made a lot of sense in an era of library-defined librarians. It also made a lot of sense when libraries, archives, and museums could guarantee employment for the graduates of library science programs. It stems from a guild model of the 1800s, when a tight interrelationship was created between institutions, the professionals who worked in them, and the programs that prepared the professionals to do so. It's a model that gave rise to accreditation of library science programs by the American Library Association, and why the association is called the "American *Library* Association," not the "American *Librarian* Association."

But the library-centered "customer" view currently makes far less sense and indeed is having a profoundly negative effect on the profession. The notion of "customers" in higher education is itself highly questionable. The relationship between students and faculty, and indeed between alums and their colleges or universities, is far more complex and mutual than one between service providers and service consumers ("customers"). As with the relationship between librarians and their communities outlined throughout this guide, students and their programs are part of each other. Thus, even though students rely on the reputation and credentials of the programs they graduate from for their first jobs, five or ten years later, the programs derive their reputations and credibility from the performance of their graduates in the field.

The profoundly negative effect caused by this view is the growing divide between library science programs and information science programs. As early as the 1970s, library science faculty saw that the value of trained "information professionals" in the banking, financial, and digital technology sectors, where information retrieval, knowledge management, and information organization were becoming increasingly important. To meet the needs of these sectors, and to make their graduates more marketable, library science programs expanded, first, to interdisciplinary library and information science programs and, later, to multidisciplinary library and information science programs that also included allied fields such as communications and computer science. Rather than expand the skill set of librarians, define that skill set outside the context of libraries, and enculturate the rapidly growing number of their students in the values of the root profession, these programs chose simply to branch out and expand to new faculty, new populations of students, and new "customers." The problem is not that the field of librarianship has expanded, but rather that, in an attempt to stay true to traditional library values, library science and information science have begun to diverge. Library science is seen as the domain of service, values, and human intermediation (including cataloging and reference). Information science has become the domain of data, technology, and automation. The problem, of course, is that librarians need to understand technology, data, and automation to best empower their community members and information professionals need to understand that systems represent values and need to empower communities..

By limiting librarians to libraries, we impede the spread of the mission and values of librarianship into other sectors of the economy and democracy. Imagine if we sent talented and ethical librarians as knowledge professionals en masse into banking, retail, computing, and government. Imagine if the apps that now pour out of Silicon Valley (and its equivalents elsewhere in the country) came from companies that valued both intellectual safety and freedom. Imagine governments at all levels committed to knowledge creation.

It's not too late to close the growing divide between library science and information science. It will take recognition of the value of librarianship by information scientists and of the value of information science by librarians. And it will take understanding on the part of those who run and manage libraries that every library position created outside a library is a gain, not a loss, that the ultimate goal of librarianship is not improved libraries, but an improved society.

Chapter 10

Although it may seem like defining what a library is makes sense for library science graduates, but not for librarians who've been in the field for years, I've found that starting conversations about community engagement with this task works extremely well for almost all librarians. At a time when libraries are adding new services and collections, both librarians and the communities they serve can become confused. How is a makerspace part of a library? What's the difference between a library and a community center?

It's important to show your librarians that these new services and collections are just a shift in the tools librarians use to accomplish their long-standing mission and to honor their values. Let them know that, with a solid footing in what a librarian is, they can be part of change at all points in their careers, but that if they define their value by what they have done day to day for as long as they've been librarians, and not by what they *can do* for their community members and for society at large, they will only resist change—and it will pass them by.

Chapter 11

The traditional reasons given for having libraries are as much myth and folklore as they are cogent arguments. I say this not because the reasons have no value or precedent, but because librarians often take them for granted. Thus, when your librarians say, "Surely everyone knows that libraries are important to democracy," remind them that (1) not everyone knows this; and (2) librarians often fail to provide specific examples of why this is so. Your librarians must work to make this and other reasons for having libraries real to the communities they serve.

Encourage them to ask—and find answers to—specific questions to that end. Has voter participation increased in the presence of active library services? Have libraries played a role in business development? Do data show student performance increases with library use? The answers to such questions can be vital in making the case for community support and participation. As data librarian extraordinaire Kimberly Silk says, "You need data and stories. The data make the stories real and the stories make the data matter."[3]

Chapter 12

It has been my experience that librarians aren't used to thinking of their libraries as platforms. They see them rather as institutions that happen to house a lot of systems (almost exclusively defined as technology systems). As a consequence, they rarely look at the entirety of the systems in their library platforms and at the impact of these combined systems on their members.

For example, your librarians might spend quite a lot of time making the web interface to the catalog work well. But, once their members find the items they want in the catalog, they then have to navigate a series of other library systems like call numbers, checkout, or interlibrary loan in order to actually get ahold of those items. By highlighting that their libraries are in fact entire systems of systems—platforms—you can help your librarians begin to see how tweaking just one library system neither solves all the problems their members may encounter, nor automatically takes into account the impact of that one system on other library systems.

As an example, early in my career, I helped build an Internet platform for educators called "AskERIC." Teachers, education students, and policy makers could go to a website and look for lesson plans and other resources. They could also send in their questions to AskERIC, and a librarian would send back answers. Early in the development of AskERIC, these two services, a website of materials and a question/answering service, were seen as distinct and separate operations, the only tie between the two being a link from one to the other.

We discovered that *where* we placed the link to ask a question on the home page actually had a direct effect on the number of questions asked. So if we placed the link on a sidebar of the home page, we received 50–60 questions a day, but if we placed it on a banner across the top of the home page, we received 200–300 questions in the same period of time. From this discovery, we could then match the number of questions asked to the amount of resources we had to answer them. By seeing these two services as part of a common platform from our members' point of view, we could ensure better service.

The goal is to get your librarians to see that all services and even "back office" operations like cataloging are connected in common library platforms. They need to break down the mental and organizational walls placed between public and technical services, or between the physical and the online presence of their libraries.

Chapter 13

Too often have I seen good ideas die at boundaries, whether between library types or between libraries and nonlibraries. Great libraries help build communities in schools, universities, towns, businesses, and beyond. Surely, academic libraries' mission of proactively speeding the scholarly conversation is not so far removed from school libraries' mission of preparing students to be critical thinkers. And don't academic, school, and public libraries all have as one of their core missions helping citizens develop knowledge so that they might actively participate in the workings of their nations? Too often have I seen librarians look to their colleagues in peer libraries not for mutual support, but for vision and direction. Too many librarians want their libraries to be second in any innovation, and, even then, only if the innovation is first carried off by a peer library that looks exactly like theirs.

I don't deny that there are key community challenges where an in-depth knowledge of libraries of the same type can be helpful. For example, urban public libraries can address issues of homelessness and economic disparities in ways private law libraries, say, simply can't. On the other hand, the best ideas on how to tackle urban issues are more likely to come from nonlibrary agencies, institutions, and organizations (social services, public interest foundations, charities, religious relief organizations) than from urban public libraries. .

The point is you need to remind your librarians that they don't strengthen our profession by talking only with their colleagues, whether in the same or different types of libraries. They strengthen our profession by reaching out for the best ideas from any source and making those ideas work for their specific communities.

Chapter 14

Academic librarians are an amazing and creative lot, but they also tend to be deeply embedded in the culture of higher education. Although some aspects of this culture are quite positive, most notably, its constant quest for learning, discovering the new, and reinterpreting the old, other aspects are stifling: hierarchy by title, rigid disciplinary boundaries, elitism, and at times, a distinct lack of empathy. This culture can lead academics to savagely attack those with different outlooks and especially those with different interdisciplinary outlooks (professors and librarians alike) and to prioritize grants and papers above engagement and change in the world around them.

I've found the greatest resistance to change in academic libraries comes in part from their librarians' belief that their role is ancillary to that of their professors, or even that they don't have a strong academic role to play. This outlook is too often learned when academic librarians encounter faculty members who have great power in their universities and who are steadfastly resistant to change.

Yet the most successful academic librarians (from community colleges to the Ivy League) see themselves as educators and have an amazing devotion to student learning. Yes, of course, they support their faculty, but they also find in students at all levels an open and willing pool of talent and promise. When all is said and done, remind your academic librarians that the way to the hearts of their faculty members and administrators alike is for them to engage their students in learning.

Chapter 15

All too often librarians of all sorts overlook the fact that libraries have prestige. With one of the most positive brands in the world, librarians have currency for engagement.[4] From iStaff teams to visiting or associate positions, your learner librarians can use positive feelings about libraries and the idea of libraries as domains of knowledge to get their members involved. It starts with volunteers knowing that, like the librarians themselves, they're serving their communities.

Chapter 16

About five years ago, there was a flood of articles in the popular press about how many librarians had tattoos. I've a theory of why all these articles appeared. Fifteen years ago, there was another flood of articles about how the Internet was going to make public libraries obsolete. Magazines and newspapers began listing these libraries as an endangered species, soon to die out. But when journalists went back to the libraries five to ten years after predicting their doom, they found them not only still there, but actually booming. Trying to make sense of this, they noticed that quite a few public librarians had tattoos and concluded that public librarians and their libraries must have become cool and hip, like the cupcake trend, and this had saved them—for now.

I contend that, as public libraries began shaping themselves more and more to the needs of their communities, they attracted more and more members, but that they did a poor job of getting this message out to the popular press and the communities themselves. It is only now that we're starting to see the popular press telling the story of how public libraries have shifted their focus and their activities to engage communities ravaged by the great recession.

Your public librarians must be concerned not only with serving their communities, but also with shaping the narrative about their communities and their work within them. Otherwise, as the communities recover, they'll have a hard time remembering the key role that public libraries played in their recovery.

FAQs (Frequently Argued Questions)

Even before *The Atlas of New Librarianship,* the ideas of this "new" librarianship generated discussion. Most of the discussions were civil, although some were downright hostile. What follows is a set of commonly raised questions, each followed by the principal argument behind it and a succinct response or clarification.

As you'll see, many of these points have already been discussed in much greater detail throughout this guide. They are distilled here for quick reference and as a refresher. Note that after "The Argument," I've put "*A* Response," not "*The* Response." I'm not claiming these are the only or even the best responses to these questions and arguments, simply the ones that have worked for me.

One last thing before we dive in. Throughout this excursus, I'm going to use the phrase "New Librarianship" as shorthand for the approach to librarianship detailed in this guide. Although I believe this approach to be simply librarianship, many will disagree; they use this phrase to distinguish this approach from previous approaches. To simplify the discussion, I've adopted their phrase.

I'm starting out with four questions from a librarian I respect a great deal: Lane Wilkinson. In preparation for a massive open online course (MOOC) on New Librarianship offered in the summer of 2013, he posted these questions on his blog.[1] I've made minor edits for the purposes of this guide. After these four are additional questions in no particular order.

"What about Fiction?"

The Argument: "If the focus of New Librarianship is on knowledge creation, where does that leave creative works such as popular fiction, music, and movies? To me, something just doesn't sound right about saying that people read *Harry Potter* or *Fifty Shades of Grey* primarily for the purposes of knowledge creation. I'm not saying that we can't or don't learn things from fiction ... of course we do. But, I don't think that's the primary reason we read novels. Maybe it's the humanities major in me, but I think New Librarianship is incomplete without an account of the role of aesthetic enjoyment, cultural enrichment, or emotional connection as encountered in creative works."

A Response: What makes us happy, what makes us sad, what disgusts or thrills us are all things we encounter in fiction and popular materials. Narratives and creative expressions, particularly the range of narratives available to us, shape our world and expand not only what we know, but what we want to know. On this, Lane and I would agree.

Now, I rephrase this question (and Lane can and will correct me if I get it wrong) to "Does every system a librarian develops or maintains (including a library) have to carry a utilitarian learning outcome?" Isn't it okay for people to go to a library just to relax, or escape or be alone? Of course it is. But the question still remains: why should a librarian devote time to make this possible? Does the community value an escape, or an aesthetic experience, or the pleasure of reading? Then it makes sense in that community to build in such services, although it might not make sense in other communities (research centers, law firms).

One of the key roles in New Librarianship is the same as in all librarianship: to provide community members with the tools they need to lead better lives. These tools can include stress reduction and entertainment as well as learning and self-improvement. The big difference here is that we must acknowledge that all communities will not place the same value on things such as fiction and popular materials, and there is nothing inherent in librarianship that requires collections of any type. Librarians build collections of tools (books, DVDs, CDs, and so on) to fulfill the goals negotiated between them and the communities they seek to serve.

That said, as discussed in chapter 4, fiction and popular materials can do so much more than simply provide a means of escape. Learning about the human condition, understanding remote cultures, humanizing the past, and even critiquing the present through fiction about the future are all possible with fiction. Games can distract, but they can also serve as vital primary sources for someone seeking to enter a gaming industry that has grown larger than the film industry of the Western world.

So should every library service have a utilitarian outcome for community members? Absolutely not. But should librarians understand the potential utility of every library service? Yes, they should.

"What about Librarians Who Don't Work in Public Services?"

The Argument: "In a widely quoted passage, Lankes claims that 'I have long contended that a room full of books is simply a closet but that an empty room with a librarian in it is a library' (*The Atlas of New Librarianship*, p. 16). In other words, the library is the librarian, not the collection. This view of the librarian as a conversation facilitator is easy to accept for librarians working in reference, instruction, makerspaces, children's libraries, and other positions where the majority of your time is spent directly interacting with patrons. But, what of the librarians in cataloging, archives, electronic resource management, web development, and other generally nonpublic facing roles within the library? If librarianship isn't about collections, what does that mean for librarians who manage collections? Basically, the New Librarian can either (1) argue that things like cataloging and archives aren't part of the future of librarianship or (2) argue that the definition of 'facilitates conversation' is broad enough to include collection-oriented library responsibilities. The first response would probably entail that librarians who work strictly with the collection aren't really librarians. I don't have to explain how problematic that response would be. The second response would require interpreting 'facilitates conversations' so broadly as to be meaningless. Where does facilitation end?"

A Response: Lane presents a false choice here: either catalogers aren't librarians or including collection building as facilitating is too broad to be useful. The reality is in between. How spaces (physical and digital), materials, and even human expertise are organized is part of librarianship, and all are part of facilitating conversations. Facilitating, by the way, doesn't mean directing them; rather, it can be creating the conditions for learning. All librarians should be creating the conditions for learning.

Will some librarians be more focused in their work (and skills) with collections? Yes. Should they work without any sense of the communities they serve? Even the most ardent traditionalist wouldn't make such an argument. All librarians have as their mission facilitating knowledge creation in their communities. Indeed, some might argue that building "metadata creation and management" through intensive knowledge of and interaction with communities has always been the goal of librarianship. S. R. Ranganathan's five laws of library science come readily to mind. Librarians have allowed themselves to become so enmeshed in tools and schemes they have failed to focus on the question of "Why?" Why do we catalog? Not so that our collections are in proper order, but so that things are discoverable. Why do we build collections of materials? To help our communities learn. This is true today; this was true in ancient Alexandria.

Too many people have sought to sideline New Librarianship as a sort of public service takeover of librarianship. Nothing could be further from the truth. Reference librarians must embrace learning over "question answering" and book genres. Acquisitions librarians must become comfortable with member-driven acquisitions as at least part of their process. System librarians must become more versed in building flexible social systems than "responsive UX systems." The world of technical service librarians is being turned on its head with linked data whose end result is neither AACR3 nor MARC 2.0, but applications that take semantics into account: the exchange of meaning—a conversation.

The bottom line is that there really are no such things as public service librarians, or reference librarians, or system librarians, or acquisitions librarians; there are just librarians who take on specific tasks and who build great expertise in them based on how well they meet the demands of knowledge development in their communities.

"What about the Autodidacts?"

The Argument: "New Librarianship is all about starting conversations within a community, and that's a good thing. But, what does New Librarianship mean for people who want to learn by themselves? Lots of research-savvy library users are perfectly content using the library without any direct intervention from the librarians on duty. Lankes does address self-directed learning insofar as he claims that conversations can happen internally for an individual. The idea being that we have an internal dialogue that counts as conversation. But, as with the definition of 'collection,' this approach seems to strain what we normally think of as 'conversation.' Basically, if the theory requires that even *thinking* is a form of conversation, then what isn't conversation and why call it 'conversation' at all? Why not just say that we gain knowledge through a combination of conversation, reasoning, observation, sensory perception, reflection, and so on?"

A Response: Much of New Librarianship is based on the way people think, as described by a whole series of dialectic learning theories. The one I use most often is conversation theory, but I could just as easily have begun with the concept of metacognition often called "critical thinking." And even though the concept of conversation could apply very widely to all things we encounter, it really applies to those things we seek to retain and incorporate into how we interact with the world. The problem is, it's impossible to know when what we learn is just for the moment and when it's for life.

An example: "What weighs six ounces, lives in a tree, and is very dangerous? A sparrow with a machine gun." That's a joke from the 1966 Batman movie I watched with my young sons. There was no pressure on me or my sons to remember the joke. Yet to this day, eight years later, any one of us can start the joke, and the other two will finish it. We learned it. We also learned it with context. We linked that agreement with our enjoyment of the movie and having fun together. So if I stretch the concept of conversation broadly, I do so because I've yet to find anyone who can limit it with fidelity.

Now on to the meat of the question: what about people who don't need the direct intervention of librarians to learn? What about them? People learn in schools, and on buses, and almost anywhere. Are there people who use libraries to learn without the direct mediation of librarians? Of course there are. The question is, why do they choose to go to a library to learn? Is it a place they find conducive to learning (for some, because it's quiet; for others, because it's loud; for still others, because they'll be near books there)? I hope so because any one of these things is the direct result of the work of librarians and the librarians' knowledge of their community.

You see, it's the combination of librarians' knowledge of learning and their knowledge of their communities that will advance the knowledge work of autodidacts or any other community members. New Librarianship is not about implementing an efficient standard system for all communities where all libraries have books and are quiet. It's about what communities need to learn and how they go about learning. Do they need makerspaces? Fishing poles? Movie collections? Librarians make choices to help their communities learn. They build spaces where autodidacts may or may not feel welcome because no space can be perfect for all learning or all people. And librarians make these choices with their communities.

"What about Noninstitutional Libraries?"

The Argument: "If it takes a librarian to make a library, then what does New Librarianship have to say about Little Free Libraries? Should we work to convince our communities to stop calling them 'libraries'? Who really decides what a library is? Communities? Librarians? Library school professors? It can get pretty tricky when you start to think about it."

A Response: Let's start with the word "library," a powerful term with a huge set of social and linguistic associations. I'm sure we're all okay with programmers calling a prebuilt collection of functions a "library." After all, there's no real confusion within or between the groups of programmers and librarians. Next, there are plenty of people who call large collections of books in their homes "libraries." Once again, I don't see any confusion here that might lead someone to break into someone else's home simply to "borrow" a book.

But what do librarians mean as professionals when we use the term "library," and how do we communicate that, when necessary, to our community members? Something like the Little Free Libraries does present a bit of a problem. Clearly, a Little Free Library doesn't meet the definition put forth in chapter 10: "A library is a mandated and facilitated space supported by the community, stewarded by librarians, and dedicated to knowledge creation." Unless, of course, it does. In some communities, librarians are part of the Little Free Library program working with their community members. Some people equip their Little Free Libraries not only with books, but also with information on library services and even "Library Boxes," small Wi-Fi hotspots to provide other information on the libraries, their locations, and more.[2]

That said, if a community can confuse what amounts to little more than a box of used books on someone's lawn with a library built and run by librarians, there's something very wrong with those librarians and the services they provide.

And who gets to decide what a library is? The ultimate answer is the community. In many states, public libraries are certified by the state through a charter. Higher education in the United States has allowed accrediting agencies to certify what an academic library is by mandating them and setting criteria for such libraries. Although librarians don't own either the term "librarian" or the term "library," we can strongly influence the meaning and use of those terms through our actions and by helping set expectations within our communities.

Isn't This Approach Too Demanding for Small Libraries?

The Argument: All this talk of publishing and software development is simply "a bridge too far" for one-librarian and other small libraries. Aren't librarians in small libraries too busy trying to buy and shelve materials to put on Human Libraries and such?

A Response: In truth, small libraries have a great advantage when it comes to implementing New Librarianship, which is all about connections to communities. The librarians of small libraries serving small communities have a greater chance to know their community members. Furthermore, small libraries need and can enlist the help of their communities to do far more than provide access to materials. They can host garden and book clubs and other important small community activities with no need for event staff. Their librarians can turn volunteer pages and shelvers into conveners and even teachers. The point of New Librarianship is not about serving big communities; it's about serving *all* communities, big, small, and in between.

This same approach, relying on the community members for support and direct contribution, also works in small libraries serving extended communities. For example, many school librarians in Canada serve large rural areas, traveling to a different school every day and making full use of student volunteers to help them provide library services. Here in the United States, when the Pine Grove Middle School was closed for renovations and its students were sent out to several other schools, Sue Kowalski had her principal buy her a used RV so that she could take the physical library to her students. Sue used each visit to reinforce her connection to them, to provide her students not just with resources, but also with the emotional and organizational support they needed to still feel part of their closed school.

New Librarianship Is Just for Public Libraries, Isn't It?

The Argument: Saying that universities and law firms are communities, too, doesn't mean that all communities are the same. The whole idea that "the community is the collection" really only applies to public libraries, doesn't it? Academic and special libraries are far too busy with activities critical to their missions to host lectures, and garden clubs, and makerspaces.

A Response: The more diverse the community, the more diverse the systems librarians build to support its aspirations. There's nothing in New Librarianship that dictates which services libraries have to offer. Librarians embedded in research or legal teams may provide a very narrow set of services, but they do so based on community participation to serve the special needs of their members while honoring the values of our profession.

But Isn't This Approach Clearly Too Radical?

The Argument: New Librarianship calls on librarians to be "agents for radical positive change," but aren't radicals almost always against the free market, consumerism, and capitalism in general?

A Response: The values of New Librarianship (service, learning, openness, intellectual freedom and safety, and intellectual honesty) are the values of librarianship itself—no more nor less. There is nothing in them that is inherently at odds with either liberal democracy or regulated capitalism. Indeed, New Librarianship has nothing against librarians working in business or librarians who are consultants to and even managers of businesses.

Quite the contrary. It supports *all* librarians who serve their communities, no matter what their communities may be, so long as they also honor the values of our profession.

That said, believing in knowledge creation and learning, we librarians must be against inequities that inhibit learning and that threaten the well-being of our communities. In order to empower our community members, we must seek out power in the form of authority and resources. At times, that will mean challenging the establishment around issues of access, knowledge, environment, and motivation. But because we serve our communities, our community members have a say in *how* we serve them. Whether a community seeks market reform or market advancement, our role as librarians is to ensure it does so in accordance with our professional values.

Why Do You Call It "New Librarianship" When It's Not That New?

The Argument: Libraries have always been about learning. That's not new. Libraries have always adopted new technologies (from tablets to scrolls to manuscripts to books to microfiches to digital documents). That's not new. Many librarians have seen things like scholarly publishing as a conversation. That's not new. Digital libraries have long talked about inclusion of communities in collection building. That's not new. Because so many of the ideas presented in this guide have been used before to talk and shape librarianship, how can you call this "New Librarianship"?

A Response: In the preface to *The Atlas of New Librarianship* I wrote: "The first thing I'd like to make clear before you read this is that I do not claim that everything in here has sprung like Athena from my head. There are some very old ideas in here. In some cases, brilliant and radical ideas that have either become lost, or so widely adopted that we have forgotten they were once radical."[3]

I learned from this never to put important things in the preface.

Is there anything in this approach to librarianship that adds to the profession or the conversation of the profession? I believe there is. The approach makes at least two major contributions that justify calling it "new." The focus on librarians and defining them without reference to the institution of a library is probably the main one. And the other is in providing a proactive and comprehensive grounding to librarianship across specific library types or functions.

Librarianship must change; it must focus on librarians to ensure not only the continuation of the profession, but also to bring the wisdom and principles of librarianship to other domains. New librarianship is not about explaining what libraries are, but about urging librarians on to renewed purpose for today's complex needs.

What about Core Functions of Libraries like Literacy and Reading?

The Argument: There are plenty of professionals in other fields who seek to improve society through knowledge creation: teachers, journalists, and publishers, to name a few. Doctors now seek not just to treat disease and injury but also to educate their patients about health. By focusing librarianship around knowledge creation and conversations, this approach makes librarianship too generic. It is the specific approaches and tools that define the profession. Cataloging, classification, and indexing have brought order to information beyond books and are at the core of librarianship. These are the skills that differentiate the profession of librarianship from other professions.

A Response: Librarians are defined by three things: our mission to improve society through facilitating knowledge creation; our means of facilitation to achieve this mission; and the values we bring to our tasks. We share each of these things separately with professionals in other fields. It is in combining all three that librarianship is unique. Furthermore, there is ample room for traditional librarian skills within the modern means of facilitation (access can still involve cataloging), but, by looking beyond the specific skills, the field has room to evolve while remaining true to its fundamental values.

All professions must evolve as their environments and the tools available to them evolve. And, to truly serve diverse communities, all professionals must adopt tools and approaches created outside their professions. If, as a librarian, you define the profession solely by tools and processes invented by librarians, you set a clear course toward obsolescence. If, on the other hand, you create a strong professional identity, you can adopt new tools and approaches from other fields and use them alongside those of traditional librarianship to better serve your community members.

Aren't You Really Describing a Community Center?

The Argument: If a library focuses on its librarians and on learning and serving its community members over its collection and facilities, how can you distinguish it from a community center filled with social services and community activities and run by nonlibrarians?

A Response: A library is not just a place with books plus 3-D printers, plus story time, plus databases, plus classes, and so on; it's an educational institution with a strong connection between its community members and its librarians. This connection and the clear dedication of its librarians to community improvement through knowledge creation sets a library apart from stand-alone makerspaces, community centers, computer clusters, and Little Free Libraries.

Also, a library is differentiated from a community center by the active role of its librarians in selecting, presenting, and preserving services (including a collection). In many ways, traditional tasks like collection development set the library apart from a community center, but collection development involves not just materials but expertise as well.

What If Our Communities Won't Accept It?

The Argument: For centuries, people have seen academic libraries as quiet spaces for scholars and the literate to do their research, and, more recently, public libraries as places of books and quiet study for everyone. How can we change this long-standing perception of libraries or establish a new social compact with our communities around this learning approach?

A Response: In Kenya, they're building as many libraries as they can. In areas too remote for construction vehicles, librarians use donkey carts to bring learning to their community members. And in the most remote northern desert areas of Kenya, they ride camels, with libraries in boxes full of mats, tents, and books strapped to their camels' backs, so they can teach mothers and children to read.

Luis Soriano packs books and teaching materials on the back of two burros to bring learning to villages deep in the forests of Colombia. In the alleys of Vancouver, British Columbia, Canadian librarians work with junkies and the homeless to show them how, through learning, they can find a job, a home, a purpose.

I could tell of librarians embedding themselves in research teams to accelerate the pace of scholarship or forming direct partnerships with doctors to improve health care, but the librarians in all of these stories have one thing in common. They did not sit by and wait to be asked; they built a new social compact by proactively engaging their communities and providing real value.

In this new social compact, librarians are respected professionals held in high esteem not because of pronouncements or association declarations, not because of any degree granted or any book written, but because of the real work we do to help make our communities better: smarter, more capable, more fulfilled.

Your Turn

This list of questions, arguments, and responses is incomplete. In fact, this approach to librarianship is incomplete. It requires you to help complete it. This approach to librarianship is a system, and all of you are its intended community. What works, what doesn't? What makes sense, what doesn't? Ultimately, our whole profession is a conversation about why we are a profession, what is our mission, and what are our means of accomplishing it.

Notes

Chapter 1

1. Egyptian Revolution of 2011," Wikipedia, last modified on August 4, 2015, https://en.wikipedia.org/wiki/Egyptian_Revolution_of_2011/.

2. Bibliotheca Alexandria, "About the BA," http://www.bibalex.org/en/Page/About/.

3. *Oxford English Dictionary*, 2nd ed., s.v., "radical." All *OED* definitions quoted in this guide are from the unabridged second edition (1989).

4. *Merriam-Webster's Collegiate Dictionary*, 11th ed., s.v. "radical."

5. Seriously, only computer scientists and drug dealers have "users." Is this really the relationship we want to have with our communities? "Please use me; I love to be used."

Chapter 2

1. *Oxford Pocket Dictionary of Current English* (Oxford: Oxford University Press, 2009), s.v. "librarian."

2. American Library Association, "Code of Ethics," http://www.ala.org/advocacy/proethics/codeofethics/codeethics/.

Chapter 4

1. Michael Buckland, "Information as Thing," unpaginated preprint Internet version of article in *Journal of the American Society of Information Science* 42, no. 5 (June 1991): 351–60, http://people.ischool.berkeley.edu/~buckland/thing.html. To be fair, Buckland really sees all three of these definitions as differing aspects of the same thing: information.

2. "DIKW Pyramid," Wikipedia, last modified on August 28, 2015, https://en.wikipedia.org/wiki/DIKW_Pyramid/.

3. For an especially imaginative way of teaching first graders addition, watch this video: Jeanne Wright, "Leprechaun Traps: Addition within 100," Teaching Channel, https://www.teachingchannel.org/videos/grade-1-math/.

4. See Common Core: State Standards Initiative, "Preparing America's Students for Success," http://www.corestandards.org/.

5. Gordon Pask, *Conversation Theory: Applications in Education and Epistemology* (New York: Elsevier, 1976).

6. Jamie Snyder, "Dialectic Theories," in R. David Lankes, *The Atlas of New Librarianship* (Cambridge, MA: MIT Press, 2011), 246–48. Snyder provides an outstanding look at dialectic theories and their connection to conversation theory in her *Atlas* agreement supplement.

7. Chimamanda Ngozi Adichie, "The Danger of a Single Story," TEDGlobal video, filmed July 2009, http://www.ted.com/talks/chimamanda_adichie_the_danger_of_a _single_story?language=en/.

8. See Michael Pollak, "The Origins of That Famous Carnegie Hall Joke," *New York Times*, November 27, 2009, http://www.nytimes.com/2009/11/29/nyregion/29fyi .html?_r=0/.

9. Bronny Fallens, *My Two Super Dads*, illustrated by Muntsa Vicente (Elwood, Australia: Little Train, 2011).

10. Leonard Susskind, "The World as a Hologram," *Journal of Mathematical Physics* 36, no. 11 (1995): 6377–96.

11. See Sam Wang and Sandra Aamodt, "Your Brain Lies to You," *New York Times*, June 27, 2008, http://www.nytimes.com/2008/06/27/opinion/27aamodt.html.

12. See "Biblioburro: The Donkey Library," PBS, July 19, 2011, http://www.pbs.org/ pov/biblioburro/.

Chapter 5

1. *Robot Test Kitchen*, blog, http://robottestkitchen.com/.

2. Joan M. Bechtel, "Conversation: A New Paradigm for Librarianship?" *College and Research Libraries* 47, no. 3 (May 1986): 219–24.

3. The Big6: Information and Technology Skills for Student Success, http://www .Big6.com/.

4. University of Rochester, "Check Out a 'Book' at the Human Library," http://www .rochester.edu/news/show.php?id=8082/.

Chapter 6

1. Clay Shirky, *Here Comes Everybody: The Power of Organizing without Organizations* (New York: Penguin Books, 2009), 14.

2. See Eli Neiburger, *Gamers ... in the Library?! The Why, What, and How of Videogame Tournaments for All Ages* (Chicago: American Library Association, 2007).

3. See Herbert A. Simon, "Rational Choice and the Structure of the Environment," *Psychological Review* 63, no. 2 (1956): 129–38.

4. Population Reference Bureau, "Traditional Families Account for Only 7 Percent of U.S. Households," March 2003,http://www.prb.org/Publications/Articles/2003/Tradi tionalFamiliesAccountforOnly7PercentofUSHouseholds.aspx

Chapter 8

1. "Life Expectancy," *Wikipedia*, last modified August 17, 2015, https://en.wikipedia. org/wiki/Life_expectancy

2. See Brewster Kahle, "A Free Digital Library," TED video, filmed December 2007, https://www.ted.com/talks/brewster_kahle_builds_a_free_digital_library?language =en/.

3. See Deborah L. Mack, *Libraries and Museums in an Era of Participatory Culture: A Partnership Project of the Salzburg Global Seminar and the [U.S.] Institute of Museum and Library Science, October 19–23, 2011*, Session 482 Report, http://www.salzburgglobal. org/fileadmin/user_upload/Documents/2010-2019/2011/482/SessionReportWeb482 .pdf/.

4. From a personal conversation with Kim.

5. On engaging as advocates those most likely to step up, see Cathy De Rosa, Jenny Johnson, and Online Computer Library Center, Inc. (OCLC), *From Awareness to Funding: A Study of Library Support in America; A Report to the OCLC Membership* (Dublin, OH: OCLC, 2008).

6. Malcolm Gladwell, *The Tipping Point: How Little Things Can Make a Big Difference* (Boston: Little, Brown, 2000).

Chapter 9

1. Andrew Carnegie, as quoted by Susan Stamberg, "How Andrew Carnegie Turned His Fortune into a Library Legacy," NPR, August 1, 2013, http://www.npr.org/2013/ 08/01/207272849/how-andrew-carnegie-turned-his-fortune-into-a-library-legacy/.

Chapter 10

1. "Five Laws of Library Science," *Wikipedia*, last modified on September 16, 2015, https://en.wikipedia.org/wiki/Five_laws_of_library_science/.

Chapter 11

1. "Information Wants to Be Free," *Wikipedia*, last modified on August 15, 2015, https://en.wikipedia.org/wiki/Information_wants_to_be_free/.

2. University of Iowa Libraries, "Local Costs of Journals," blog entry by Wendy Robertson, February 16, 2012, http://blog.lib.uiowa.edu/transitions/?p=720&utm_source=dlvr.it&utm_medium=twitter/.

3. Texas State Library and Archives Commission, "Facts at a Glance," last modified on June 24, 2015, https://www.tsl.texas.gov/texshare/facts_ataglance.html.

4. Freegal Music, "About Freegal Music," http://www.freegalmusic.com/homes/aboutus—Check out the Librarian in Black for a perspective on the service: http://librarianinblack.net/librarianinblack/just-say-no-to-freegal/.

5. Indiana Business Research Center, *The Economic Impact of Libraries in Indiana* (Bloomington: Indiana University, Kelley School of Business, 2007), http://www.ibrc.indiana.edu/studies/EconomicImpactofLibraries_2007.pdf/.

6. Nicole Steffen et al. (2009), Public Libraries—A Wise Investment: A Return on Investment Study of Colorado Libraries (Denver: Library Research Service), v, http://www.lrs.org/documents/closer_look/roi.pdf/.

7. G José-Marie Griffiths, Donald W. King, and Thomas Lynch. (2004), Taxpayer Return on Investment in Florida Public Libraries: Summary Report (Tallahassee: Florida Dept. of State, State Library and Archives), figure 1, http://roi.info.florida.gov/Content/PDFs/Studies/Library%20ROI%202004.pdf/.

8. Indiana Business Research Center (2007), The Economic Impact of Libraries in Indiana (Bloomington: Indiana University, Kelley School of Business), 5. http://www.ibrc.indiana.edu/studies/EconomicImpactofLibraries_2007.pdf/.

9. José-Marie Griffiths et al. (2006), Taxpayer Return-on-Investment (ROI) in Pennsylvania Public Libraries (Chapel Hill: University of North Carolina, School of Information and Library Science).

10. University of South Carolina, School of Library and Information Science (2005), The Economic Impact of Public Libraries on South Carolina (Columbia: University of South Carolina, School of Library and Information Science), 5, http://www.libsci.sc.edu/sceis/final%20report%2026%20january.pdf/.

11. Marianne Kotch (2006–2007), The Economic Value of Vermont's Public Libraries, 2006–2007 (Montpelier: State of Vermont, Department of Libraries).

12. NorthStar Economics, Inc. (2008), The Economic Contribution of Wisconsin Public Libraries to the Economy of Wisconsin (Madison: NorthStar Economics), 7, http://pld.dpi.wi.gov/sites/default/files/imce/pld/pdf/wilibraryimpact.pdf/.

13. University of North Carolina at Charlotte Urban Institute (2010), Expanding Minds, Empowering Individuals, and Enriching Our Community: A Return on Investment Study of the Charlotte Mecklenburg Library (Charlotte: University of North Carolina at Charlotte Urban Institute), 24, 47, http://ui.uncc.edu/sites/default/files/pdf/Library_ROI_Study_2010_Final_FullReport.pdf/.

14. Carnegie Mellon University Center for Economic Development. (2006). Carnegie Library of Pittsburgh: Community Impact and Benefits (Pittsburgh: Carnegie Mellon University Center for Economic Development), 10, http://www.clpgh.org/about/economicimpact/CLPCommunityImpactFinalReport.pdf/.

15. Glen E. Holt, Donald Elliott, and Amonia Moore (1999). Placing a Value on Public Library Services, "Results of the SLPL Study," http://www.slpl.lib.mo.us/libsrc/resresul.htm/.

16. Levin, Driscoll & Fleeter. (2006). Value for money: Southwestern Ohio's return from investment in public libraries. Retrieved from http://9libraries.info/docs/EconomicBenefitsStudy.pdf

17. Pearl M. Kamer (2005). *Placing an Economic Value on the Services of Public Libraries in Suffolk County, New York* (Bellport, NY: Suffolk Cooperative Library System), 2, http://scls.suffolk.lib.ny.us/pdf/librarystudy.pdf/.

18. Andrew Albanese, "Survey Says Library Users Are Your Best Customers," *Publisher's Weekly*, October 28, 2011, http://www.publishersweekly.com/pw/by-topic/industry-news/publishing-and-marketing/article/49316-survey-says-library-users-are-your-best-customers.html.

19. Megan Oakleaf, *The Value of Academic Libraries: A Comprehensive Research Review and Report* (Chicago: Association of College and Research Libraries, 2010), http://www.ala.org/acrl/sites/ala.org.acrl/files/content/issues/value/val_summary.pdf/.

20. Denise M. Davis, John Carlo Bertot, and Charles R. McClure, *Libraries Connect Communities: Public Library Funding and Technology Access Study, 2007–2008*, ed. Larra Clark (Chicago: American Library Association, 2008), http://www.ala.org/research/sites/ala.org.research/files/content/initiatives/plftas/previousstudies/0708/LibrariesConnectCommunities.pdf/.

21. "Destruction of the Library of Alexandria," *Wikipedia*, last modified on September 2, 2015, https://en.wikipedia.org/wiki/Destruction_of_the_Library_of_Alexandria/.

22. See Judi Dench, "Spaceship Earth," YouTube video, April 29, 2012, https://www.youtube.com/watch?v=8cUJbbB4kOk/.

23. Ray Oldenburg, *Celebrating the Third Place: Inspiring Stories about the "Great Good Places" at the Heart of Our Communities* (New York: Marlowe, 2001).

24. Jefferson to Edward Carrington, Paris, January 16, 1787, *The Works of Thomas Jefferson*, 12 vols., ed. Paul Leicester Ford (New York: G. P. Putnam's Sons, 1904), 5:252–53, http://oll.libertyfund.org/titles/jefferson-the-works-vol-5-correspondence-1786-1789/.

25. Andrew Carnegie, as quoted in American Library Association, "Quotable Quotes about Libraries," http://www.ala.org/PrinterTemplate.cfm?Section=Available_PIO_Materials&Template=/ContentManagement/HTMLDisplay.cfm&ContentID=11968/.

26. Madison to W. T. Barry, August 4, 1822, *The Writings of James Madison*, 9 vols., ed. Gaillard Hunt (New York: G. P. Putnam's Sons, 1900–1910), 9:103, http://press-pubs.uchicago.edu/founders/documents/v1ch18s35.htm/.

27. Library of Congress, THOMAS database, http://thomas.loc.gov/home/thomas.php/.

28. U.S. National Library of Medicine, PubMed database, http://www.ncbi.nlm.nih.gov/pubmed/.

29. See Carnegie Foundation for the Advancement of Teaching, "Foundation History," http://www.carnegiefoundation.org/who-we-are/foundation-history/.

30. Barbara Quint, "I in the Sky: Visions of the Information Future 'Marchers in Time,'" *Searcher: The Magazine for Database Professionals* 8, no 1 (January 2000), http://www.infotoday.com/searcher/jan00/quint.htm/.

Chapter 12

1. John G. Palfrey has a beautiful discussion of the dangers of nostalgic attachment to libraries in his excellent book *BiblioTech: Why Libraries Matter More Than Ever in the Age of Google* (New York: Basic Books, 2015).

2. See Free Library of Philadelphia, "History of the Free Library of Philadelphia," http://www.freelibrary.org/about/history.htm/.

3. On the dangers of overreliance on digital resources, see *roytennant.com:Digital Libraries Columns*, "Avoiding Unintended Consequences," blog entry by Roy Tennant, January 1, 2001, http://roytennant.com/column/?fetch=data/77.xml/.

Chapter 13

1. To get a sense of the information literacy debate among academic librarians, see Lane Wilkinson's take on "threshold concepts," *Sense and Reference: A Philosophical Library Blog*, "The Problem with Threshol Concepts," entry by Lane Wilkinson, June 19, 2014, https://senseandreference.wordpress.com/2014/06/19/the-problem-with -threshold-concepts/.

Chapter 15

1. One of the best examples of a school library website is the one created by teacher-librarian Joyce Valenza at the Springfield Township High School in Erdenheim, Pennsylvania: http://springfieldlibrary.wikispaces.com/.

2. See, for example, David Abel, "Welcome to the Library. Say Goodbye to the Books: Cushing Academy Embraces the Digital Future," *Boston Globe*, September 4, 2009, http://www.boston.com/news/local/massachusetts/articles/2009/09/04/a _library_without_the_books/.

3. See, for example, Welcome to TouchCast in (and outside) the Classroom, Which We Like to Call EduCast, http://www.touchcast.com/education/.

4. Buffy Hamilton, http://quartz.syr.edu/blog/?page_id=7653/.

5. See *The Unquiet Librarian*, "First Efforts at Written Conversations Strategies Write-Around Text on Text," blog entry by Daniel Cinchetti, Jennifer Lund, and Buffy Hamilton, December 20, 2013, https://theunquietlibrarian.wordpress.com/2013/ 12/20/first-efforts-at-written-conversations-strategies-write-around-text-on-text/. See also Harvey Daniels and Elaine Daniels, *"Write-Arounds": The Best-Kept Teaching Secret; How Written Conversations Engage Kids, Activate Learning, Grow Fluent Writers, K–12* (Thousand Oaks, CA: Corwin Literacy, 2013), 155–91.

6. Texas State Library and Archives Commission, "School Library Progams: Standards and Guidelines for Texas," last modified March 2, 2011, https://www.tsl.texas .gov/ld/schoollibs/sls/stand4.html.

Chapter 16

1. In a few countries, publicly funded libraries directly support other publicly funded institutions such as government agencies. Although the general public may be the ultimate beneficiary of services provided by these libraries, the effect is often indirect. For most purposes, such "special libraries" are not normally part of the conversation on public libraries. But I'll have more to say about special libraries in chapter 17.

2. See Colbe Galston et al., "Community Reference: Making Libraries Indispensable in a New Way," *American Libraries*, June 13, 2012, http://americanlibrariesmagazine .org/2012/06/13/community-reference-making-libraries-indispensable-in-a-new -way/.

3. Peter Bromberg, Personal conversation.

Facilitating New Librarianship Learning

1. Fred Rogers, http://www.fredrogers.org/about/beginnings/.

Observations from the Field

1. See R. David Lankes, "Mapping Conversations," in *The Atlas of New Librarianship* (Cambridge, MA: MIT Press, 2011), 107–11.

2. See David Ferriero, "Going Forward," 2015 IMLS Focus: National Digital Platform, Session 8, YouTube video, published May 14, 2015, https://www.youtube.com/ watch?v=-ZuLJUGSzAw/.

3. See Kimberly Silk's biography, http://kimberlysilk.com/about/quotefrompersonal conversation.

4. On libraries' currency for engagement, see Kathryn Zickuhr, Kristen Purcell, and Lee Rainie, "From Distant Admirers to Library Lovers—and Beyond," Pew Research Center, report, published March 13, 2014, http://www.pewinternet.org/2014/03/13/ library-engagement-typology/.

FAQs (Frequently Argued Questions)

1. These four questions and the original arguments can be found on Lane Wilkinson's excellent blog *Sense and Reference*, https://senseandreference.wordpress .com/2013/07/08/new-librarianship-and-open-questions/.

2. See The LibraryBox Project, http://librarybox.us/.

3. R. David Lankes, preface, in *The Atlas of New Librarianship* (Cambridge, MA: MIT Press, 2011), xi.

Discussion Points

Chapter 1

1. Why in times of crisis do people protect or support their libraries?
2. What would you, as a professional librarian, do in a situation like the protests in Ferguson, Missouri? How would you support peaceful protests? What would do about violent riots?
3. How did Melvil Dewey seek to redefine librarianship? What contributions did S. R. Ranganathan make to how we see libraries?
4. What do we call those we serve as librarians? How do we determine the right term or phrase?

Chapter 3

1. Can there by one field-wide mission for librarianship? Why or why not?
2. Can librarians and individual libraries have separate missions? How do the two relate? What happens when they conflict?
3. Can a librarian be neutral and unbiased? Explain your position.
4. "The mission of librarians is to improve society through facilitating knowledge creation in their communities." What other professions and groups can claim this as their mission? How can librarians partner with them? How do librarians compete with them?

Chapter 4

1. Is fiction an important component of knowledge development? Explain why or why not.

2. Can one classification system represent global knowledge? Explain your position. Can you find other examples in the Dewey Decimal System that represent a particular view of the world?

3. What is information?

4. What is the role of "truth" in librarianship?

5. Can you give examples of books that have been interpreted in very different ways by different people?

6. Can you think of other topics where an answer could be interpreted as biased or where providing multiple points of views could give undue weight to alternative points of view?

7. Do librarians have a responsibility to present multiple points of view on a topic? How might that change how a member or a community sees that topic?

8. Can you give examples in your own experience where people held simplistic ideas about you, your background, or your ideas?

9. Can you identify words that have unique meanings in particular times, places, cultures, or situations?

10. What are the implications of source amnesia for the services librarians offer?

Chapter 5

1. We have said librarians are educators, does that mean they are also teachers? Is it worthwhile making this distinction? Why or why not?

2. What other nonbook collections can you think of to serve specific communities? Where's the line between the work of a librarian and the work of a museum professional or, for that matter, a warehouse manager?

3. What other forms of community expertise exist in local citizens, scholars, businesspeople, or professionals?

4. How can librarians promote and ensure civil discourse both in the spaces they mediate and in the spaces hosted by others (like social media)?

5. What are some ways of motivating community members to learn?

6. When can a librarian do more good than harm by removing privacy protections in certain services and systems?

Chapter 6

1. Can you recall a particularly effective class you've taken? Did it allow for participation and conversation? How?
2. How can libraries use the social nature of communities to build better systems? How can systems you use on a regular basis (digital and non-digital) benefit from conversation?
3. Can you identify different subcommunities you're a part of? What are the competing values and demands of these subcommunities?

Chapter 7

1. When can giving community members what they want actually hurt the members or the larger community? How do you decide between helping your members or your community?
2. Do you agree that all literacies have a common root? Are media literacy, information literacy, and reading literacy all part of the same thing?
3. Should librarians seek to accumulate power? How and why?
4. How do the different types services librarians offer either reinforce or weaken existing power structures? Should librarians always seek to weaken power structures? Why or why not?
5. What contexts limit the openness of librarians?
6. Are there environments where community interest trumps a member's right to privacy?
7. What are other ways to view the world besides the scientific, rationalist approach? How do these worldviews clash with or complement one another?

Chapter 8

1. What's the best way to instill the values of the profession in librarians by hire?
2. How does the hiring nonlibrarians affect the culture of libraries?
3. What are some local collections that make sense? In what ways can librarians tailor collections to the needs of their local communities?

4. Can you give examples where using local culture (language, references, traditions) would have helped or did help serve a community?
5. Can you give examples of innovation on the local level that you've made happen or that you've witnessed?

Chapter 10

1. "A library is a mandated and facilitated space supported by the community, stewarded by librarians, and dedicated to knowledge creation." Is this definition sufficiently broad to encompass all libraries? Is it too broad? Explain your position.
2. What are some ways communities enact mandates for libraries?
3. What other ways do librarians mediate community member interactions without being directly involved?
4. Can you give examples of libraries changing services, systems, or facilities over time? How were these changes tied to changes in the community?

Chapter 11

1. For what other reasons would a library offer Freegal?
2. In what ways do libraries actively encourage and support learning?
3. How is the idea that history is both important and a matter of interpretation represented in libraries?
4. What are some other examples of how popular interpretations of history have changed over time? What role can libraries play in shaping these interpretations?
5. How can libraries act as community spaces apart from their physical facilities? Is there a fear that libraries will be seen as *just* community spaces with no value attached to the mediation of their librarians? If there is, say why it might or might not be justified.
6. How does a library represent community aspirations in its architecture and location? Is the library still the heart of a community, whether town, city, school, or university? Should it be?

Chapter 12

1. Can a nostalgic view of libraries actually hinder the work of librarians?
2. A long-standing argument is that having common services across all libraries of a given type is a good way to help communities. Librarians gain economies of scale, and community members know what to expect from a library no matter what community they travel to. How would you support or counter this argument? What other institutions use this logic?
3. What are some of your personal passions and how could you build a library program around them?
4. How can you instill a sense of ownership in your library in your community members? How can you demonstrate that your community has ownership in the first place?

Chapter 13

1. What are some physical systems that still use reductionist classification to make items browsable?
2. Is there value to providing a common face or service across all libraries or all libraries of a given type?

Chapter 14

1. What are some of the modes of scholarly communications and how are they changing? Do these new nodes expand or curtail conversations within and across disciplines?
2. Do all academic librarians need a research agenda? Does this apply to teaching colleges and community colleges? Explain why or why not.
3. How else can librarians bring real problems into the classroom and academy?

Chapter 15

1. How do librarians advance structured curricula in schools? How do they augment them? When should they seek to change them?

2. How can volunteer programs provide librarians with more time for community engagement?

3. How can school libraries be both refuges and spaces for engagement?

Chapter 16

1. How have the justification for and mission of public libraries changed over time?

2. How can you promote the idea that the boundaries of a library extend to where librarians do their work, not just to where the library's physical space stops?

3. In what ways can long-standing library services be reconceptualized in the community approach to librarianship?

4. Is the role of libraries as places where members can gather and build their communities on an ongoing basis valued and supported? Can you name other places besides libraries where they can do this?

5. Can you give examples of libraries going beyond the mandates of their communities?

Additional Reading

Chapter 3

Casson, Lionel. (2001). *Libraries in the Ancient World*. New Haven: Yale University Press.

Lankes, R. David. (2011). "Mission." In *The Atlas of New Librarianship*, 14–29. Cambridge, MA: MIT Press.

Chapter 4

Ford, Nigel. (2004). "Modeling Cognitive Processes in Information Seeking: From Popper to Pask." *Journal of the American Society for Information Science and Technology* 55 (9): 769–82.

Lankes, R. David. (2008). "Credibility on the Internet: Shifting from Authority to Reliability." *Journal of Documentation* 64 (5): 667–86.

Lankes, R. David. (2011). "Knowledge Creation." In *The Atlas of New Librarianship*, 31–64. Cambridge, MA: MIT Press.

Pask, G. (1976). Conversation Theory: Applications in Education and Epistemology. New York: Elsevier.

Talja, Sanna, Kimmo Tuominen, and Reijo Savolainen. (2005). "'Isms' in Information Science: Constructivism, Collectivism and Constructionism." *Journal of Documentation* 61 (1): 79–101.

Wilkinson, Lane. (2011). For a strong opposing point of view to Talja, Tuominen, and Savolainen's approach to knowledge, read Wilkinson's blog entries on constructivism: https://senseandreference.wordpress.com/2011/05/18/libraries-are-not-in-the-construction-business/.

Wilson, Patrick. (1983). *Second-Hand Knowledge: An Inquiry into Cognitive Authority*. Westport, CT: Greenwood Press.

Chapter 5

Antoni, Giacomo. (2009). "Intrinsic vs. Extrinsic Motivations to Volunteer and Social Capital Formation." *Kyklos* 62 (3): 359–70.

Arnone, Marilyn P., Ruth V. Small, Sarah A. Chauncey, and H. Patricia McKenna. (2011). "Curiosity, Interest and Engagement in Technology-Pervasive Learning Environments: A New Research Agenda." In "Motivation and New Media" (special issue). *Education Technology Research and Development* (*ETR&D*) 59 (2): 181–98.

Information literacy. For an academic library view, see http://www.ala.org/acrl/issues/infolit/intro/. And for a school library view, see http://aasl.ala.org/essentiallinks/index.php?title=Information_Literacy/.

Lankes, R. David. (2011). "Facilitation." In *The Atlas of New Librarianship*, 65–81. Cambridge, MA: MIT Press.

Mardis, Marcia A., Ellen S. Hoffman, and Todd E. Marshall. (2008). "A New Framework for Understanding Educational Digital Library Use: Re-Examining Digital Divides in U.S. Schools." *International Journal on Digital Libraries* 9 (1): 19–27.

Small, Ruth V. (1998). "Motivational Aspects of Library and Information Skills Instruction: The Role of the Library Media Specialist." In Daniel Callison, Joy McGregor, and Ruth V. Small, eds., *Instructional Interventions for Information Use*, 11–15. San Jose, CA: Hi Willow Research.

Chapter 6

Lankes, R. David. (2011). Systems discussion and "Communities." In *The Atlas of New Librarianship*, 35–39, 53–62 and 83–115, respectively. Cambridge, MA: MIT Press.

Simon, Herbert A. (1956). "Rational Choice and the Structure of the Environment." *Psychological Review* 63 (2): 129–38.

Simon, Herbert A. (1957). *Models of Man: Social and Rational*. New York: Wiley.

Chapter 7

Alinsky, Saul D. (1971). *Rules for Radicals: A Practical Primer for Realistic Radicals*. New York: Random House.

Gee, James Paul (1992). *The Social Mind: Language, Ideology, and Social Practice*. Series in Language and Ideology. New York: Bergin & Garvey.

Gee, James Paul (1999). *An Introduction to Discourse Analysis: Theory and Method*. London: Routledge.

Lankes, R. David. (2011). "Improve Society." In *The Atlas of New Librarianship*, 117–36. Cambridge, MA: MIT Press.

McCook, Kathleen de la Peña. McCook's writings are seminal on social justice issues. For her list of selected publications, see http://shell.cas.usf.edu/~mccook/selectedpublications.htm/.

Chapter 8

Lankes, R. David. (2011). "Librarians." In *The Atlas of New Librarianship*, 137–85. Cambridge, MA: MIT Press.

Lankes, R. David. (2012). "Salzburg and a Few of My Favorite Things." In *Expect More: Demanding Better Libraries for Today's Complex World*, 993–96. Jamesville, NY: Riland Press.

Palmer, Katherine, Kevin Stolarick, and Kimberly Silk. (2014). "So Much More: The Economic Impact of the Toronto Public Library on the City of Toronto." Survey. http://www.slideshare.net/ksilk/so-much-more-the-economic-impact-of-toronto-public-library-on-the-city-of-toronto/.

Salzburg Curricular Framework. See http://quartz.syr.edu/blog/wp-content/uploads/2014/12/Salzburg1.pdf/.

Chapter 10

Lankes, R. David. (2012). "The Mission of Libraries: Expect More Than Books." In *Expect More: Demanding Better Libraries for Today's Complex World*, 27–39. Jamesville, NY: Riland Press.

Chapter 11

Buschman, John. (2007). "Democratic Theory in LIS [Library and Information Science]: Toward an Emendation." *Journal of the American Society for Information Science and Technology* 58 (10): 1483–96.

Lankes, R. David. (2012). "The Argument for Better Libraries: Expect Impact." In *Expect More: Demanding Better Libraries for Today's Complex World*, 9–25. Jamesville, NY: Riland Press.

Oldenburg, Ray. (2001). *Celebrating the Third Place: Inspiring Stories about the "Great Good Places" at the Heart of Our Communities*. New York: Marlowe.

Palmer, Katherine, Kevin Stolarick, and Kimberly Silk. (2014). "So Much More: The Economic Impact of the Toronto Public Library on the City of Toronto." Survey.

http://www.slideshare.net/ksilk/so-much-more-the-economic-impact-of-toronto
-public-library-on-the-city-of-toronto/.

Chapter 12

Lankes, R. David. (2012). "Communities: Expect a Platform." In *Expect More: Demanding Better Libraries for Today's Complex World*, 75–86. Jamesville, NY: Riland Press.

Palfrey, John G. (2015). *BiblioTech: Why Libraries Matter More Than Ever in the Age of Google*. New York: Basic Books.

Weinberger, D. (2012). "Library as Platform." *Library Journal*, August 15. http://lj.libraryjournal.com/2012/09/future-of-libraries/by-david-weinberger/#_/.

Chapter 13

Lankes, R. David (2007). "Library Association 2.0." *Searcher Magazine*, September, 50–53.

Lankes, R. David. (2011). "Leadership." In *The Atlas of New Librarianship*, 132–34. Cambridge, MA: MIT Press.

Sullivan, Doreen. (2015). For more examples of skew in the Dewey Decimal System, see Sullivan's "A Brief History of Homophobia in Dewey Decimal Classification." *Overland*, July15. http://overland.org.au/2015/07/a-brief-history-of-homophobia-in-dewey-decimal-classification/.

Chapter 14

Bonn, Maria, and Mike Furlough, eds. (2015). *Getting the Word Out: Academic Libraries as Scholarly Publishers*. Chicago: Association of College and Research Libraries. http://www.ala.org/acrl/sites/ala.org.acrl/files/content/publications/booksanddigitalresources/digital/9780838986981_getting_OA.pdf/.

Kendrick, Curtis, and Irene Gashurov. (2013). "Libraries in the Time of MOOCs." *Educause Review*, November 4. http://www.educause.edu/ero/article/libraries-time-moocs/. Although just about everything about MOOCs will be dated by the time you read this, Kendrick and Gashurov have some good points to think about.

Lankes, R. David. *On Productivity: Introducing a Blog Series on Reinventing the Academic Library*. http://quartz.syr.edu/blog/?p=6510/. Many of the public services that academic libraries can provide were first posted on my blog and elicited some great feedback.

Chapter 15

Crow, Sherry R., and Ruth V. Small. (2011). "Developing the Motivation Within: Using Praise and Rewards Effectively." *School Library Monthly* 27 (5): 5–7.

Eisenberg, Mike B., and Robert E. Berkowitz. (1994). "The Big Six." Poster. Syracuse, NY: 2–212 Center for Science & Technology.

Fontichiaro, Kristin, Buffy Hamilton, R. David Lankes, and Diane Cordell. (2011). *School Libraries: What's Now, What's Next, What's Yet to Come.* eBook. Los Gatos, CA: Smashwords.

Hamilton, Buffy (2011). "School." In R. David Lankes, *The Atlas of New Librarianship*, 368–70. Cambridge, MA: MIT Press.

Loertscher, David V. (2012). "Get an iTeam in Your Life and See the Difference!" *Teacher Librarian*, December. http://cnyric.myschoolpages.com/schools/ESM/files/news/iamistaff.pdf/.

Stripling, Barbara K. (2014). "Advocating for School Librarians." *American Libraries* 45 (1/2): 6.

Stripling, Barbara K. (2014). "Reimagining Advocacy for School Libraries." *American Libraries*, Digital Supplement on School Libraries, 8–13.

Valenza, Joy Kasman, Brenda L. Poyer, and Della Curtis. (2014). "Social Media Curation." *Library Technology Reports* 50 (7).

Chapter 16

Galston, Colbe, Elizabeth K. Huber, Katherine Johnson, and Amy Long. (2012). "Community Reference: Making Libraries Indispensable in a New Way." *American Libraries* 43 (5/6): 46–51. http://americanlibrariesmagazine.org/2012/06/13/community-reference-making-libraries-indispensable-in-a-new-way/.

Index